Crafts for All Seasons

pil

Publications International, Ltd.

ISBN: 1-4127-0033-7

Library of Congress Control Number: 2003109993

Contents

Fall 85

Winter 119

Index 160

Tips and Techniques

Need something to keep you busy on a rainy spring day? Having trouble finding that perfect gift for everyone on your holiday list? Then open up the pages of *Crafts for All Seasons,* and start crafting!

Divided into the seasons of the year, this book offers many exciting crafts that take a day or less to create. The projects featured use a wide variety of techniques and methods. You'll find everything from traditional crafts to those that take advantage of today's new materials and techniques. We've included projects for all skill levels. Each one has complete step-by-step instructions and photos to help make everything easy to understand and fun to do. However, the basic information that follows will help you get started.

Before plunging into any project, read the directions thoroughly. Check to make sure you have all the materials needed. Many of the items you need may be on hand already. Your local craft store will probably be a good source for other materials.

Next, read the basic information in this section for the craft you'd like to make. These pages will define terms, help you choose materials, and describe certain techniques that are essential to that craft.

General Pattern Instructions

When a project's instructions tell you to cut out a shape according to the pattern, trace the pattern from the book onto tracing paper with a pencil. If the pattern has an arrow with the word *FOLD* next to a line, it is a half pattern. Fold a sheet of tracing paper in half, then open up the paper. Place the fold line of the tracing paper exactly on top of the fold line of the pattern, and trace the pattern with a pencil. Then refold and cut along the line, going through both layers. Open the paper for the full pattern.

Some of the patterns in this book are printed smaller than actual size. You will have to enlarge them on a photocopier before using them, copying the pattern at the percentage indicated near the pattern.

TRANSFERRING DESIGNS

You don't have to know anything about drawing to transfer a design. The designs in this book can be transferred directly onto the project surface.

Transfer supplies: tracing paper, tape, pencil or fine marker, transfer paper (carbon or graphite), stylus

1. Place transparent tracing paper over the design you want to copy. Tape a few edges down to hold the pattern in place. Trace the design lines with a pencil or fine marker. Trace only the lines you absolutely need to complete the project.

2. Place a piece of transfer paper, carbon side down, between the surface and the pattern. Choose a color that will easily show on your project, and use a stylus or pencil to trace over the design lines. Lift a corner of the pattern to make sure the design is transferring properly.

Sewing

Before plunging into a sewing project, check to make sure you have all the materials needed. Most of the items you need will probably be on hand already.

BASIC SUPPLIES

Fabrics

The type of fabric best suited to the project is given in the list of materials. But don't hesitate to make substitutions, taking into consideration your preferences in colors and patterns. Keep in mind the scale of a pattern relative to the size of the project. The weight of the fabric is an important consideration: Don't substitute a heavy, stiff fabric for a delicate one.

Scissors

Two styles are needed, one about 8 to 10 inches long with a bent handle for cutting fabric. This style of scissors allows you to cut through the fabric while the fabric lays flat. These shears should be sharp and used only for fabric. The second style of scissors is smaller, about 6 inches, with sharp points. You will need this style for smaller projects and close areas.

Straight pins

Nonrusting dressmaker pins are best to use because they will not leave rust marks on your fabric if they come in contact with dampness or glue. They also have very sharp points for easy insertion.

Tape measure

This should be plastic coated so it won't stretch and can be easily cleaned.

Ironing board and steam iron

Be sure your ironing board is padded and has a clean covering. Sometimes you do more sewing with the iron than you do with the sewing machine. Keeping your fabrics, seams, and hems pressed cuts down on stitches and valuable time. It is important to press your fabric to achieve a professional look. The iron is also used to adhere fusible interfacing. Keep the bottom of your iron clean and free of any substance that could mark your fabric. The steam iron may be used directly on most fabrics with no shine. Test a small piece of the fabric first. If it causes a shine on the right side, iron on the reverse side.

Thread

Have mercerized sewing thread in the colors needed for each project you have chosen. Proper shade and strength (about 50 weight) of thread avoids having the stitching show more than is necessary and will give the item a more finished look.

Fusible webbing (or adhesive)

A lightweight fusible iron-on adhesive is timesaving and easy to use. The webbing is placed paper side up on the wrong side of the material. Place iron on paper side of adhesive, and press for 1 to 3 seconds. Allow fabric to cool. The design can then be drawn or traced onto the paper side and cut out. Remove the paper, place the material right side up in the desired position on the project, and iron for 3 to 5 seconds.

Sewing machine

Neat, even stitches are achieved in very few minutes with a sewing machine. If desired, you may machine-stitch a zigzag stitch around the attached fusible adhesive pieces to secure the edges.

Work surface

Your sewing surface should be a comfortable height for sitting and roomy enough to lay out your projects. Keep it clean and free of other crafting materials that could accidentally spill or soil your fabric.

Quilting

This section will help you familiarize yourself with quilting techniques—both modern and old-fashioned—and materials. You can use this basic knowledge to make the quilts in this book or to create your own original masterpieces.

BASIC SUPPLIES

Fabric

In general, it is worth investing in the best materials you can afford. Many inexpensive fabrics are less likely to be colorfast. Try to select only 100% cotton fabrics for the face and back of the quilt. Cotton is easy to cut, mark, sew, and press. It is also widely available. Fabrics that contain synthetics, such as polyester, are more difficult to handle and are more likely to pucker.

Top: Warm colors. Bottom: Cool colors.

For the most part, you should select colors of 1 type—either bright or pastel—to use in one quilt. Consider using cool colors such as purple, blue, and white or warm colors such as yellow, orange, red, and off-white. Sometimes a fabric that seems light by itself is very dark next to other fabrics. To avoid this, look at all the fabrics you plan to use through a red transparent report cover (available in most stationery stores). Do the fabrics you thought were dark look dark next to the ones you thought were light? Do you mix light and dark fabrics? Does this create the effect you are trying to achieve?

Use prints with a variety of scales or all with the same scale. That is, use large prints, medium prints, and small prints in the same quilt or use only large, medium, or small prints. If you use all small prints with one large-scale print, the large-scale print will probably look out of place.

Left: Large, medium, and small prints. Right: Three small prints.

When you have selected fabrics, buy a small amount of each (no more than ¼ yard). Cut out enough of each fabric to make up 1 block. Evaluate the block. Are you happy with all the fabrics and how they work together? Step back and look at the block from a distance. Does it still look good? This is the time to make changes to your fabric selection if necessary. Be sure you do it right away, while the material is still in the store.

The backing fabric should be similar in fiber content and care to the fabrics used in the quilt top. Some wide cottons (90 and 108 inches) are sold specifically for quilt backings. They eliminate the need to piece the back. As you work on quilts, it's a good idea to keep a scraps basket rather than discarding unused fabric. Some quilts call for very small amounts of fabric for appliqués. If you can find the right color among your scraps, you'll save yourself the trouble and waste of purchasing ⅛ yard of fabric for a much smaller piece.

Batting

In general, use polyester batting with low or medium loft. For a puffier quilt, use high-loft batting, but consider tying the quilt (see page 14), since this batting is difficult to quilt. Polyester is better if the quilt will be washed frequently. Cotton batting is preferred by some quilters for a very flat, traditional-looking quilt. Wool batting is a pleasure to quilt and makes a warm cover.

Thread

It may seem tempting to use up old thread on a quilt. However, working with old, weak thread is frustrating because it can often become tangled and knotted. Consider buying 100% cotton thread or good long-staple polyester thread for piecing, appliqué, and machine quilting. Use monofilament nylon thread (.004mm or size 80) for freehand machine quilting. Cotton quilting thread is wonderful for hand quilting but should not be used for machine quilting because it is stiff and will tend to lie on the surface of the quilt.

For piecing by hand or by machine, select a neutral color thread that blends in with most of the fabrics in the quilt. For most projects, either khaki or gray thread works well. Use white thread for basting; do not risk using colored thread that may leave color behind. For appliqué, the thread should match the fabric that is being applied to the background. The color of quilting thread is a personal design choice. If you want your stitching to show up, use a contrasting thread color.

Scissors

A sharp pair of scissors is essential for quilting. Ideally, set aside a pair of scissors to be used on fabric only. Paper and plastic quickly dull the cutting edges of scissors, so keep a separate pair for cutting out templates and other non-fabric items.

Rotary cutter, see-through ruler, and self-healing mat

These tools let you cut strips of fabric efficiently. If you become very involved with quilting, you may find that a collection of cutters, mats, and rulers of different sizes and shapes is valuable. A good starter set would include the large-size cutter, a 6×24-inch ruler, and a mat at least 22 inches wide.

Marking tools

Most fabrics can be marked with a hard-lead pencil. Mechanical pencils are worthwhile investments because they are always sharp. A special fabric eraser can help remove light pencil markings. Other handy marking tools include colored pencils designed for marking on fabric and a fine-tip permanent pen for signing your finished quilt. Soapstone pencils make a light mark that is easy to brush off, but they lose their sharp point quickly and must be sharpened often. Tailor's chalk or chalk wheels are helpful for marking quilting patterns just before you quilt. The chalk brushes off fabric easily. Disappearing-ink pens may

Quilting supplies: a) quilting hoop, b) self-healing mat, c) see-through ruler, d) rotary cutter, e) darning foot, f) even-feed walking foot, g) quilter's thimble, h) sharp, i) scissors, j) betweens, k) safety pins, and l) template plastic.

be tempting because they make a mark that is easy to see, but heating fabric that contains residue from the ink can create a permanent stain. Leaving a work in progress in a hot car or in a sunny window can cause this to happen. Consider banning this risky product from your quilting basket.

Template plastic

Traditionally, templates were made of scrap cardboard. Cardboard is satisfactory, although if a template is going to be used many times, template plastic is better because it does not wear down. It is available as plain white sheets or transparent sheets printed with a grid.

Quilting needles

The needles used for hand piecing and hand appliqué are called *sharps*. For hand quilting, use *betweens* (quilting needles). Generally, start with a size 8 and work toward using a size 10 or 12. Use the smallest needle you can to make the smallest stitches.

Always use a sharp needle on your sewing machine; a dull needle will tend to skip stitches and snag the threads of your fabric, creating puckers. Use size 9/70 or 11/80 for piecing and appliqué and size 11/80 (in most cases) or 14/90 (for a thick quilt) for machine quilting.

Straight pins

Use fine, sharp straight pins (such as silk pins) for piecing and holding appliqué pieces in place before basting or stitching. Long quilter's pins are used to hold the 3 layers (top, batting, and backing) before they are basted together or quilted. Have a large box of safety pins (size 2) on hand for basting when machine quilting.

Quilting hoop or frame

If you plan to quilt by hand, you need some way of holding the area you are stitching smooth. Some people do this successfully with their hands, but most quilters prefer to use a quilting hoop or quilting frame. Quilting hoops are portable and inexpensive. A small area of the quilt is surrounded by the hoop, which keeps the fabric taut. For large bed quilts, many quilters prefer to use a quilting frame, which supports the entire quilt, with large areas available for quilting at any given time. However, quilting frames are a significant investment and require space. Consider using quilting hoops until you feel the need to work on a quilting frame. All the projects in this book can be completed successfully with a hoop. Experiment with different styles to see what feels most comfortable.

Steam iron and ironing board

You will need a handy steam iron and ironing board. To streamline your workflow, place the ironing board at right angles to the sewing table and raise it to the same height. This arrangement will allow you to press seams after they are stitched without getting up.

Sewing machine

Quilts can, of course, be made entirely by hand. Today, however, many quilters do all their piecing—and some do all their quilting—by machine. The machine does not have to make lots of fancy stitches. However, it does need to stitch an accurate ¼-inch seam with an even tension.

Material Preparation

Prewashing

Always wash fabrics first. This will remove some of the chemicals added by the manufacturer and make it easier to quilt. Also, cotton fabric does shrink, and most of the shrinkage will occur during the first washing and drying. Be sure to use settings that are as hot as those you intend to use with the finished quilt.

Dark, intense colors, especially reds, tend to bleed or run. Wash these fabrics by themselves. If the water becomes colored, try soaking the fabric in a solution of 3 parts cold water to 1 part white vinegar. Rinse thoroughly. Wash again. If the fabric is still losing its color, discard the fabric and select another. It is not worth using a fabric that may ruin the other fabrics when the finished quilt is washed.

Marking and cutting fabric

To cut fabric the traditional way for piecing or appliqué, place the pattern on the wrong side of the fabric. Trace around the template with a hard-lead pencil or a colored pencil designed for marking on fabric. If the template does not include a seam allowance, add one. Cut around each piece with sharp fabric scissors.

In many cases, it is faster and easier to cut fabric using a rotary cutter. This tool, which looks and works like a pizza cutter, must be used with a self-healing mat and a see-through ruler. Always employ the safety shield of the rotary cutter when it is not in use.

Fold the fabric in half lengthwise with the selvages together. Adjust one side until the fabric hangs straight. The line created by the fold is parallel to the fabric's straight of grain. Keeping this fold in place, lay

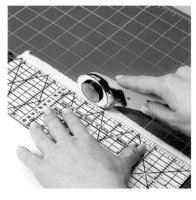

the fabric on the mat. Place a see-through ruler on the fabric. Align a grid line on the ruler with the fold, and trim the uneven edge. Apply steady, even pressure to the rotary cutter and to the ruler to keep them and the fabric from shifting. Do not let the

cutter get farther away from you than the hand that is holding the ruler. Stop cutting and reposition your hand. Reposition the ruler so that it covers the width of the strip to be cut and the trimmed edge is on the markings for the appropriate measurement on the ruler.

After cutting the strip, hold it up to make sure it is straight. If it is angled, refold the fabric and trim it again. Continue cutting strips, checking frequently that the strips are straight.

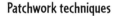

Patchwork techniques

Unless otherwise noted, all seam allowances for projects in this book will be ¼ inch.

Accuracy is important. A small error repeated in each block or, worse yet, in each seam, will become a large distortion. Before starting a large project, make a sample block and measure it. Is it the desired size? If not, figure out where the inaccuracy occurred. Are any seams a few threads too wide or narrow? Clip seams and restitch.

Hand piecing

With right sides together, align fabric pattern pieces so that the ends of the seam match. (Use straight pins to check.) Pin the seam. Make sure the seam lines match exactly.

Cut a piece of thread approximately 18 inches long. Put the end that came off the spool of thread first through the eye of the needle. Knot the other end, using a quilter's knot. To make a quilter's knot, wrap the end of the thread around the tip of the needle (wrapping from the base toward the point of the needle) 3 times. Then pull the needle through the wraps. Pull the knot down to the end.

Stitch from one end of the seam to the other, using a running stitch (about 8 stitches per inch). For additional strength, backstitch at the beginning and end of each seam. Do not stitch across the seam allowance. In general, press the seam toward the darker fabric.

Machine piecing

When machine piecing, set your sewing machine's stitch length to 10 to 12 stitches per inch (or between 2 and 3 on machines that do not use the stitches per inch measure). Stitch across the seam allowance, along the

seam line, and across the seam allowance at the far end of the seam. Do not backstitch.

Make sure the seam allowance is consistently ¼ inch. The presser foot on a few sewing machines is a true ¼ inch. Stitch a sample, and then measure the seam

allowance. If you are off by just a hair on each piece you stitch, the errors will accumulate, and the end result may be distorted.

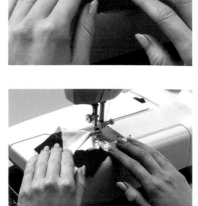

If your sewing machine does not have a mark or a ¼-inch-wide presser foot, place several layers of masking tape to act as a sewing guide. Make a sample and measure it for accuracy.

Piecing curves

Fold each curved piece in half to find the center of the seam. Clip the concave curve ³⁄₁₆ inch deep approximately every ³⁄₁₆ inch along the curve

(clip more often for a very tight curve, less often for a gradual curve). With the 2 pieces' right sides together, match the center of each seam and the end points. Pin carefully. With the concave curve on top, stitch the pieces slowly, easing the fabric so that the edges stay even.

Chain piecing

To streamline the sewing of multiple units, use chain piecing. Stitch a seam, and then without removing that unit from the sewing machine, insert the next unit to be stitched. Continue stitching from one unit to the next. Make as many units as practical in one long chain. Then snip the threads connecting the units and press each unit. During the course of a project, this technique can save a substantial amount of time.

Strip piecing

Strip piecing is another technique that can save lots of time when making quilts with complex blocks. Instead of using templates, cut strips of fabric. (Use a rotary cutter and a ruler for the greatest efficiency.) Stitch the strips of fabric together.

Then cut the strips and recombine the resulting units. See individual projects for specific instructions.

Hand appliqué

Prepare pieces of fabric to be appliquéd by hand by tracing around the template on the right side of the fabric. Add a 3/16-inch seam allowance as you cut out each piece. Fold under the seam allowance along the marked seam line. Baste around each piece to hold the seam allowances turned under, clipping curves where necessary.

Pin the first piece to be stitched to the background.

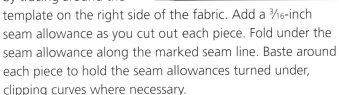

Hand-stitch it to the background with a blind stitch, or, for a more decorative look, use a blanket stitch and contrasting thread.

When the appliqué is complete, consider carefully trimming the background fabric from behind the appliqué

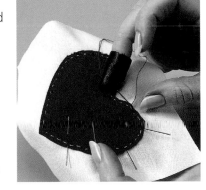

inside the stitching line. This must be done with great care so that the appliqué is not snipped, but it does reduce the bulk and make quilting easier.

Machine appliqué

For machine appliqué, there is no seam allowance added to pattern pieces. Use fusible webbing to hold the appliqué firmly in place. Follow the manufacturer's instructions to iron fusible webbing to the wrong side of the appliqué fabric. Trace the pattern piece on the paper side of the fusible webbing, cut out the appliqué, and follow the manufacturer's instructions to bond it to the background fabric. (For the quilts in this book, always place the pattern piece faceup on the paper side of the fusible webbing to trace the appliqué shape, unless otherwise instructed.) Stitch around the appliqué using a 1/8-inch- to 3/16-inch-wide zigzag stitch. The stitches should be close together, but not so close that the fabric does not feed smoothly through the machine.

FINISHING TOUCHES

Assembling the quilt top

For a traditional quilt, arrange the completed quilt blocks. Sew the blocks together to form rows. Press. Sew the rows together. For quilts not made up of blocks, follow instructions for the individual projects to assemble.

Pressing

Press completed quilt blocks from the back first and then lightly from the front. Do not apply pressure because this may stretch and distort the fabric. Instead, rely on lots of steam.

Press the completed quilt top before basting it to the batting and backing. Do not press a quilt once the batting has been added, because this will flatten it.

Adding borders

Add borders that are not quilt pieces simply by sewing strips of fabric (of the desired width) to the long sides of the quilt. Trim the ends of the strips even with the short sides of the quilt. Then

stitch strips of fabric to the short sides, stitching across the borders previously applied.

Press the borders and the seam allowances away from the center of the quilt. If there is more than 1 border, apply the borders in the same order for each.

In certain quilts, mitered corners, which require a little more time and care, look better than square or butted corners. To miter corners, find the center of each border strip and the center of each side of the quilt. One side at a time, pin the border and stitch, beginning and ending ¼ inch from the edge of the quilt top. (Borders need strips longer than the sides for mitering.)

With right sides together, fold the quilt top diagonally, taking care to match seams and the edges of the borders. Use a ruler and pencil to extend across the border strips to the line formed by the fold.

Taking care not to snag seam allowances, stitch from the inside edge of the border to the outer corner on the marked line. Trim the ends of the border strips and press the seam open. Repeat for each corner.

Finishing the outer edges

Decide how you will finish the outer edges of your quilt before you prepare for quilting. Traditionally, the outer edges of quilts are encased in binding after the quilt is quilted. The binding wears better than other options, so the time spent applying the binding is worth it if you want

the quilt to last a long time. Binding techniques are described on pages 14–15.

Some faster techniques, however, are done before the quilt is quilted. They include placing the right sides of the quilt top and backing together over the batting and stitching around the outside edges, leaving an opening through which the quilt is turned. Then the opening is slipstitched closed.

Preparation for quilting

Decide what designs the quilting stitches will make. For a traditional look, outline important elements of the design with quilting. A grid of stitching works well in background areas. Fancier design elements that complement the theme of the quilt can also be incorporated. Make sure that there will be some stitching every few inches to secure the batting so it does not shift.

Decide now if you need to mark the top for quilting. Simple outlining for grids can be marked with masking tape as you quilt. For more elaborate quilting designs, mark the top with one of the marking tools described on pages 7–8. Use the lightest mark possible. Dark marks may be difficult to remove when the quilt is finished.

Spread out the backing (right side down) on a table or other flat surface. Use masking tape to secure the backing after smoothing it out. Place the batting on top of the backing, smoothing it out also. Finally, place the completed quilt top on the backing, right side up. Stretch it out so it is smooth, and tape it.

For hand quilting, baste the layers together using long stitches. Start basting at the center of the quilt and work toward the edges. Create a grid of basting by making a line of stitching roughly every 4 inches.

For machine quilting, baste by hand as described previously or use safety pins. Place a safety pin every 3 or 4 inches. In order to save time later, avoid placing pins on quilting lines.

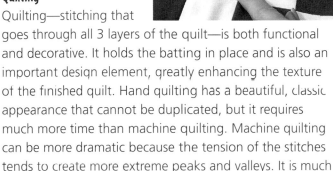

Quilting

Quilting—stitching that goes through all 3 layers of the quilt—is both functional and decorative. It holds the batting in place and is also an important design element, greatly enhancing the texture of the finished quilt. Hand quilting has a beautiful, classic appearance that cannot be duplicated, but it requires much more time than machine quilting. Machine quilting can be more dramatic because the tension of the stitches tends to create more extreme peaks and valleys. It is much faster and wears well.

To outline design areas, stitch ¼ inch away from each seam line. Simply decide where to stitch by eye, or use ¼-inch masking tape placed along each seam as a guide. Masking tape can also be used as guides for straight lines and grids. Stitch beside the edge of the tape, avoiding stitching through the tape and getting adhesive on the needle and thread. Do not leave the masking tape on the fabric when you are finished stitching each day, however, because it can leave a sticky residue that is difficult to remove.

Hand quilting—Some quilters hold their work unsupported in their lap when they quilt. Most quilters, however, prefer to use some sort of quilting hoop or frame to hold the quilt stretched out. This makes it easier to stitch with an even tension and helps to prevent puckering and tucks. Use *betweens* (quilting needles) for hand quilting. The smaller the needle (higher numbers such as 11 and 12), the easier it will be to make small stitches. A quilting thimble on the third finger of your quilting hand will protect you from needle sores.

Use no more than 18 inches of quilting thread at a time. Longer pieces of thread tend to tangle, and the end gets worn as it is pulled through the fabric. Knot the end of the thread with a quilter's knot. Slip the needle into the

quilt top and batting about an inch from where the first stitch should start. Pull the needle up through the quilt top at the beginning of the first stitch. Hold the thread firmly and give it a little tug. The knot should pop into the batting and lodge between the quilt top and backing.

The quilting stitch is a running stitch. Place your free hand (left hand for right-handed people; right hand for left-handed people) under the quilt to feel for the needle as it pokes through. Load the needle with a couple of stitches by rocking the needle back and forth. At first, focus on making evenly sized stitches. Also, make sure you are going through all three layers. When you have mastered that, work on making the stitches smaller on future quilts.

Machine quilting—Machine quilting is easy to learn, but it does take some practice. Make a few trial runs before starting to stitch on your completed quilt. On the test swatch, adjust the tension settings for the machine so the stitches are even and do not pucker or have loose loops of thread.

The easiest machine stitching is long straight lines, starting at the center of the quilt and radiating out. These lines may be in a grid, stitched in the ditches formed by seams, outlines around design elements, or channels (long, evenly spaced lines).

Whatever the pattern, quilt from the center to the outer edges. Plan the order of stitching. Your plan should minimize the need to start and stop as much as possible. Before placing the quilt on the sewing machine, roll the sides in toward the center and secure the rolls with pins or bicycle clips. Use an even-feed walking foot for straight lines of stitching. For freehand stitching, use a darning foot and lower the feed dogs or use a throat plate that covers the feed dogs.

To begin, turn the handwheel to lower and raise the needle to its highest point. Pull gently on the top thread to bring the bobbin thread up through the quilt. Stitch in place for several stitches. Gradually increase the length of each stitch for the first ½ inch of quilting until the stitches are the desired length. This will secure the ends of the threads, making it unnecessary to backstitch or knot them. Reverse these steps at the end of each line of quilting.

When quilting with the even-feed walking foot, place your hands on either side of the presser foot and apply an even pressure. Keep the layers smooth and free of tucks.

When doing freehand quilting, place your hands around the darning foot and apply gentle outward pressure to keep the layers smooth. Guide the fabric with smooth, even motions of the wrist. In freehand quilting, the fabric is free to move in any direction; it is not fed through the machine by the feed dogs. The stitch length is

determined by the speed of the needle and the motion of the fabric under the needle. To keep the stitches the same length, maintain a steady speed and even motions. It takes some practice to get smooth curves and even stitch lengths using this technique, so don't be discouraged if your first attempts are a bit rough.

Tying quilts

The fastest way to secure the layers of a quilt (top, batting, and backing) together is to tie them. Thread a needle with a long piece of embroidery floss, yarn, or pearl cotton. At regular intervals (every 4 inches, at

most) take a single stitch through the 3 layers of quilt. Tie the thread in a double square knot, and trim the thread to a consistent length, usually ½ or 1 inch.

If you prefer, you can tie your quilt by machine. Baste as usual. Place the quilt on the machine and make sure all the layers are smooth. Set the stitch length and width at 0. Take several stitches, then increase the stitch width to a wide setting. Make about 8 stitches, and return the stitch width to 0. Make several stitches, and clip the threads. Repeat until the quilt is tied at regular intervals.

To make the ties more decorative, make little bows from 6-inch lengths of ribbon and stitch them in place, using the zigzag stitch as just described. Alternately, if your machine makes decorative stitches, use a decorative stitch instead of the zigzag stitch.

Binding

Binding may be made from strips of fabric that match or coordinate with the fabrics used in the quilt. These strips may be cut on the straight grain or on the bias. Straight binding is easier to cut and apply and can be used on most of the projects in this book. Quilts that have curved edges require bias binding. Also, bias binding is stronger and tends to last longer. You can also purchase quilt binding and apply it according to the manufacturer's instructions.

To make straight binding, cut strips of fabric 3¼ inches wide (or follow directions for individual quilts) on the lengthwise or crosswise grain. For each side of the quilt you will need a strip the length of that side plus 2 inches. For example, if the side measures 40 inches long, cut your strips 42 inches long.

Baste around the quilt ¼ inch from the outer edge. Make sure all corners are square, and trim any excess batting or fabric. Prepare each strip of binding by folding it in half lengthwise, wrong sides together, and press. Find the center of each strip. Also find the center of each side of the quilt.

Place the binding strip on top of the quilt, aligning the raw edges of the strip and of the quilt and matching the centers. Stitch a ½-inch seam from one end of the quilt to the other. If you use an even-feed walking foot instead of the regular presser foot, it will be easier to keep the binding and the quilt smooth.

Trim excess binding from each end. Fold the binding to the back of the quilt, and slipstitch it in place. Repeat for the opposite side of the quilt. Attach the binding to the other two sides of

the quilt using the same procedure, but do not trim the ends of the binding. Instead, fold the excess binding over the end of the quilt. Holding the end in place, fold the binding to the back of the quilt and slipstitch in place.

Making a hanging sleeve

To make a sleeve for hanging a quilt, cut a strip of fabric (muslin or a scrap of backing fabric) 6 inches wide and as long as the quilt is wide. To finish the ends of the strip, roll under the ends to the wrong side of the fabric and slip-stitch (or machine-stitch). Fold the fabric lengthwise with wrong sides together. Stitch a ⅜-inch seam the length of the sleeve. Turn the sleeve wrong side out and press the seam. Stitch a ⅝ inch seam over the first seam. Turn the sleeve right side out, and press. Stitch the sleeve to the top of the quilt and insert a dowel to hang the quilt.

Making a label

All quilts should have a label with the quilter's name and date. Years after a quilt was made and its original purpose forgotten, it is exciting to discover that the maker documented the occasion with information such as why and for whom the quilt was made. Consider putting your thoughts and feelings on a label for each quilt.

Labels can be elaborate displays of needlework done in embroidery or counted cross-stitch, or they can be quick and simple. Use colored pens and calligraphy to get fancier. A leftover block makes a nice label. Write on it with a permanent pen and then appliqué it to the back of the quilt.

Cross-Stitch

Cross-stitch is traditionally worked on an even-weave cloth that has vertical and horizontal threads of equal thickness and spacing. The cloth can have as few as 5 threads to the inch or as many as 22. The most common even weave fabric is 14-count Aida cloth, meaning it has 14 threads to the inch. Designs can be stitched on any fabric count—the resulting size of the project is the only thing that will be affected. Since the count number refers to the number of stitches per inch, the smaller the count number of the fabric, the larger the design will be. Thus a design worked on 14-count fabric will be half the size of the same design worked on 7-count fabric.

Six-strand embroidery floss is used for most stitching. Many other beautiful threads, particularly metallic threads, can be used to enhance the appearance of the stitching.

BASIC SUPPLIES

Needles

A blunt-end or tapestry needle is used for counted cross-stitch. The recommended size for most stitching is a #24 needle.

Hoops

You can use an embroidery hoop while stitching—just be sure to remove it when not working on your project, since it will leave an imprint on the material.

Scissors

A small pair of sharp scissors is a definite help when working with embroidery floss.

Floss

Six-strand cotton embroidery floss is most commonly used, and it's usually cut into 18-inch lengths for stitching. Use 2 of the 6 strands unless the directions for that project tell you otherwise. Also use 2 strands for backstitching, unless the directions state otherwise.

PREPARING TO STITCH

Directions for the cross-stitch project in this book will tell you the size of the piece of cloth you need to complete the project.

Position the center of the design in the center of the fabric. To locate the center of the fabric, lightly fold it in half and in half again. Find the center of the chart by following the arrows on the side and top.

Reading the chart is easy—each square on the chart equals 1 stitch on the fabric. Near each chart you will find a color key listing the colors used and showing a representative square of each color. Select a color, and stitch all of that color within an area. Begin by holding the thread ends behind the fabric until secured or covered over with 2 or 3 stitches. You can skip a few stitches on the back of the material to get from one area to another, but do not run the thread behind a section that will not be stitched in the finished piece—it will show through the fabric.

If your thread begins to twist, drop the needle and allow the thread to untwist. It is important to the final appearance of the project to keep an even tension when pulling stitches through so that all stitches will have a uniform look. To end a thread, weave or run the thread under several stitches on the back side. Cut the ends close to the fabric.

Horizontal rows

Cross all stitches in the same direction. Work the stitches in 2 steps—first do all the left-to-right stitches (bringing your needle up at 1 and down at 2), and then go back over them to do all the right-to-left stitches (bringing your needle up at 3 and down at 4).

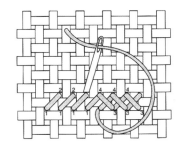

Vertical rows

Work each complete stitch before going on to the next stitch, bringing your needle up at 1, down at 2, up at 3, and down at 4.

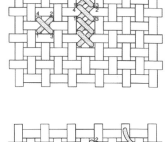

Backstitch

Outlining and creating letters is often done in backstitch, which is shown by bold lines on the patterns. Your needle comes up at 1 and all odd-numbered holes and goes down at 2 and all even-numbered holes. Backstitch is usually worked after the pattern is completed.

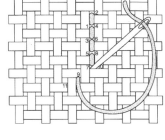

Making Wreaths

The wreaths featured in this book have been created for you to make, and we encourage you to duplicate them. We also urge you to come up with wreath designs of your own. Before you begin, you should have some supplies and tools on hand.

BASIC SUPPLIES

Scissors

Fabric scissors will be used for cutting ribbons and fabrics. Keep them handy; you will reach for them often. Also keep on hand a pair of heavy-duty scissors for cutting other items, such as florals, thin wire, or other craft items. Don't mix up the scissors—use the fabric scissors on fabric only to keep them sharp.

Wire cutters

These are used for cutting silk flower stems, floral wire, and other objects that cannot be cut by scissors. Wire cutters can also be used to cut small branches and stems of dried flowers. Garden clippers are also useful to have on hand for clipping heavier branches and stems.

Needlenose pliers

Use these to grasp materials that your fingers cannot. They are also helpful when twisting heavier gauge wire.

Craft knife

While not an essential tool, a craft knife can come in handy. Use it in place of scissors to cut materials such as corrugated cardboard or foam.

Floral wire

Floral wire comes in many gauges. The higher the gauge number, the finer the wire. You'll use 16-gauge wire to make a hanger for your wreath, while you'll want to use finer wire (18- and 20-gauge wire) for strengthening flower stems. The finer gauges can be used when you are making bows. Wire is sold in straight lengths as well as on spools and paddles. If it is to be used for stems, straight lengths are best. Wrap the finer spool or paddle wire around clusters or groupings of smaller materials when attaching them to a wreath or garland.

Floral tape

This is a waxy crepe paper that will stick only to itself when stretched. It is available in many colors. Choose the shade closest to the materials you are working with (you may need several different colors for the same wreath), and use it to cover stems and to reinforce wire floral picks.

Wire floral picks

Made of wood and available in several lengths, floral picks are used to reinforce or lengthen stems that you will insert in floral or plastic foam or into a straw wreath.

U-shape pins

These are also known as pole, craft, or floral pins. Use them to attach materials to foam or straw wreaths.

Tweezers

Tweezers are occasionally needed to handle small items, especially when you are working with hot glue.

Glue

Most wreath projects will call for craft glue or a glue gun. Regardless of which glue gun you use, work quickly once you have applied the melted glue. The glue loses its adhesiveness as it cools. Hold the glued object in place for a few seconds while the glue cools. When you're done

gluing, you may find many fine webs of glue hanging from your completed wreath. Use tweezers to remove them from fragile dried materials. If you find them in a wreath made with sturdier materials, such as a pinecone wreath, use a handheld hair dryer to melt them away.

Hanging a Wreath

In most cases, you will add a hanger to a wreath frame before you add the materials. Make sure the hook is on the back of the wreath, and be sure the wreath hangs flat on your door or wall before continuing with the wreath. It's harder to fix any problems after the wreath has been assembled. Following are a couple different hanger options.

Chenille stem hanger

Use only on wreaths covered with materials that will conceal this hanger. To make one, bend a 12-inch length evenly into a U. Twist the U end into a 1- or 2-inch oval loop. Wrap and twist the ends around the wreath tightly, positioning the loop at the top. Apply hot glue to twisted end to reinforce.

You can use the same technique to wrap the chenille stem tightly around a wire wreath form or a grapevine wreath, placing it far enough down the back so it is not visible from the front. Wrap the chenille stem with floral tape so it is easier to hide. You can also use a length of a medium-weight wire taped with floral tape. Covering a wire hanger with floral tape will help prevent scratch marks on the door or wall.

Wire loop hanger

Use only on straw or plastic foam wreaths. Bend 6 inches of heavy floral wire into a U. Twist the U end into a 1-inch oval loop. Bend the cut ends at right angles to the loop and push into the foam or straw until the loop is flush with the wreath. Secure to the wreath with hot glue placed on the bent end of the hanger.

A Word About Glue

Glue can be a sticky subject when you don't use the right one for the job. There are many different glues on the craft market today, each formulated for a different crafting purpose.

GLUE TYPES

White glue

This may be used as an all-purpose glue—it dries clear and flexible. It is often referred to as craft or tacky glue. Tacky on contact, it allows you to put 2 items together without a lot of setup time required. Use it for most projects, especially ones involving wood, plastics, some fabrics, and cardboard.

Thin-bodied glues

Use these glues when your craft project requires a smooth, thin layer of glue. Thin-bodied glues work well on some fabrics and papers.

Fabric glue

This type of glue is made to bond with fabric fibers and to withstand repeated washing. Use this glue for attaching decorations to fabric projects. Some glues require heat-setting. Check the bottle for complete instructions.

Hot-melt glue

Formed into cylindrical sticks, this glue is inserted into a hot-temperature glue gun and heated to liquid state. Depending on the type of glue gun used, the glue is forced out through the gun's nozzle by either pushing on the end of the glue stick or squeezing a trigger.

Use clear glue sticks for projects using wood, fabrics, most plastics, ceramics, and cardboard. When using any glue gun, be careful of the nozzle and the freshly applied glue—they are very hot! Apply glue to the piece being attached. Work with small areas at a time so that the glue doesn't set before being pressed into place.

Low-melt glue

This is similar to hot-melt glue in that it is formed into sticks and requires a glue gun to be used. Low-melt glue is used for projects that would be damaged by heat, such as foam, balloons, and metallic ribbons.

Decorative Painting

There are a wide variety of paint brands to choose from. Acrylic paints are available at your local arts and crafts stores. This type of paint dries in minutes and allows projects to be completed in no time at all. Clean hands and brushes with soap and water.

Some projects may require a medium that is not acrylic or waterbase. These require mineral spirits to clean up. Always check the manufacturer's label before working with a product so you can have the proper cleaning supplies on hand.

VARNISHES

Choose from a wide variety of varnishes to protect your finished project. Varnish is available in either brush on or spray. Brush-on waterbase varnishes dry in minutes and clean up with soap and water. Use over any acrylic paint. Don't use over paints or mediums requiring mineral spirits to clean up. Spray varnishes can be used over any type of paint or medium. Varnishes are available in matte, satin, or gloss finishes. Choose the finish you prefer.

BRUSHES

Foam (sponge) brushes

These work well to seal, basecoat, and varnish surfaces. Clean foam brushes with soap and water when using acrylic paints and mediums. For paints or mediums that require mineral spirits to clean up, you will have to throw away the disposable brush.

Synthetic brushes

Use with acrylic paints for details and designs. You will use a liner brush for thin lines and details. A script brush is needed for extra long lines. Round brushes are used to fill in round areas, for stroke work, and to make broad lines. An angle brush is used to fill in large areas, float, or side load color. A large flat brush is used to apply basecoat and varnish. Small flat brushes are for stroke work and basecoating small areas.

WOOD PREPARATION

Properly preparing your wood piece so it has a smooth surface to work on is important to the success of your project. Once the wood is prepared, you are ready to proceed with a basecoat, stain, or finish.

Supplies you will need to prepare the wood: sandpaper (#200) for removing roughness; tack cloth, which is a sticky, resin-treated cheesecloth to remove dust after sanding; wood sealer to seal wood and prevent warping; and foam or 1-inch flat brush to apply sealer.

BASIC PAINTING TECHNIQUES

Thin lines

1. Thin paint with 50 percent water for a fluid consistency that flows easily off the brush (about ink consistency).

2. Use a liner brush for short lines and tiny details or a script brush for long lines. Dip brush into thinned paint. Wipe excess on palette.

3. Hold brush upright with handle pointing to the ceiling. Use your little finger as a balance when painting. Don't apply pressure for extra thin lines.

Spattering

The spatter-paint technique is used to create little dots of paint sprinkled on a surface—great for creating snow or an aged flyspeck look or for just adding fun colors to a finish. Always test spattering on scrap paper first.

1. Thin paint with 50 to 80 percent water. Use an old toothbrush and a palette knife, or use a Kemper tool. Dip brush into thinned paint. Lots of paint on the brush will create large dots. As paint runs out, dots become finer.

2. With a toothbrush, drag your thumb or palette knife across the top of the bristles causing them to bend. As they are released, the bristles spring forward, spattering the paint onto the surface.

Dots

Perfectly round dots can be made with any round implement. The size of the implement determines the size of the dot. You can use the wooden end of a paintbrush, a stylus tip, a pencil tip, or the eraser end of pencil (with an unused eraser).

Use undiluted paint for thick dots, or dilute paint with 50 percent water for smooth dots. Dip the tip into paint and then onto the surface. For uniform dots, you must redip in the paint for each dot. For graduated dots, continue dotting with the same paint load. Clean tip on paper towel after each group, and reload.

Bows and Ribbons

There are many ways to make bows, and the more you make, the easier it becomes. Cutting the ends of a ribbon at an angle lends a more polished appearance to the finished product.

Multiloop Bow

1. Unroll several yards from a bolt of ribbon. Form loops from ribbon with your dominant hand. Pinch center of loops with thumb and forefinger of your other hand as you work.

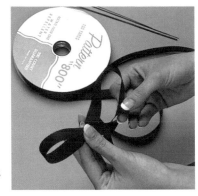

2. Continue to add loops to your bow. Keep pinching the bow's center with your thumb and forefinger. After you have all the loops you desire, trim away excess ribbon from the bolt. If you want a streamer, leave the ribbon longer before cutting.

3. Insert a length of wire around the center of the ribbon. Bring the 2 wire ends securely and tightly next to the bow's center to eliminate loop slippage. Attach the bow to your project with the wire. You can also trim the wire and glue the bow in place.

Note: When using heavier ribbon, use a chenille stem to secure the bow. The tiny hairs on the stem will hold the bow securely and not allow potential twisting of the bare wire. For tiny, delicate bows, thin cloth-covered wire can be used for securing. It eliminates slipping and is so tiny that it disappears into the bow loops.

E-Z Bow

1. This bow is added directly to a wreath. Cut the desired number of ribbon lengths to make the streamers. Angle- or V-cut streamer ends. Crimp the streamers in the middle, and attach them to the wreath with a floral pin.

2. Cut the desired number of ribbons to make individual clustered loops; angle- or V-cut the ends of each piece.

To make a cluster, fold the end of one strip 6 inches with wrong sides together. Crimp the ribbon midway at 3 inches, and continue folding and crimping to the end of the ribbon length. Place a floral pin over the crimped center, and attach it to the wreath above the streamers. Repeat for all ribbons.

3. Place the individual clusters in a tight group. Fluff the loops to conceal the pins.

Spring

The signs of spring—robins, tulips, budding trees, and warmer weather—lift our spirits after a long winter.
So why wait for spring outside when you can create spring inside even during the coldest days? Take advantage of those April showers, and start crafting!

Spring Garden Wall Hanging

*Spring has sprung in this delightful scene.
Simple appliqué techniques will help you quickly make this
colorful wall hanging, providing a burst
of warm sunshine in any season.*

What You'll Need

- Tracing paper
- Pencil
- Scissors
- 1 yard fusible webbing
- Iron and ironing board
- See-through ruler
- Self-healing mat
- Rotary cutter
- ½-inch bias tape maker (optional)
- Fabric scissors
- Straight pins
- Sewing machine
- Quilting needles
- Matching thread
- 22×27 inches cotton batting
- 4 black beads, 4mm each
- 2 yellow buttons, ⅝ inch each

Appliqué fabrics

- 6-inch squares: 1 each bright yellow print, bright pink print, bright red print, dark red print, tan-and-black check, medium green print
- 4-inch squares: 1 each dark purple print, light purple print, bright blue print
- 5-inch squares: 1 each brown check, dark brown print
- 2½-inch squares: 1 each medium purple print, bright blue print, black
- 8-inch square dark green print
- 1×8 inches brown

Quilt fabrics

- ¼ yard each light blue print, green flower print, light green print, light yellow print, medium blue print, light tan print, light brown print
- 15½-inch squares: 1 each olive green print, dark green print
- ⅛ yard brown print
- 22×27 inches backing
- ¼ yard dark brown

1. Trace and cut out all patterns on pages 26–27. Iron fusible webbing to wrong side of all appliqué fabrics. Trace all appliqué shapes on paper side of fusible webbing, referring to finished quilt illustration on page 25 to match shapes to fabric squares.

2. From light blue print, cut one 5½×10½-inch rectangle. From green flower print, cut two 5½-inch squares. Cut one 5½-inch square from light green print. From light yellow print, cut

one 5½-inch square. Cut one 5½-inch square and one 5½×15½-inch rectangle from medium blue print. From light tan print, cut one 5½×10½-inch piece.

3. From 15½-inch olive green print square, cut four 1-inch-wide strips on the bias. If you are using a bias tape maker, follow manufacturer's instructions to fold and press each long side ¼ inch to wrong side to make ½-inch bias strip. If you are not using a tape maker, use iron to fold and press each long side ¼ inch to wrong side. Fold and press two of the strips in half to make ¼-inch bias tape. From 15½-inch dark green print square, cut two 1-inch-wide strips. As with olive strips, make ¼-inch bias tape from both strips.

Tip

Instead of making your own bias tape, you may purchase premade bias tape.

4. To make block 1, trace and cut out sunflower, sunflower center, and 3 leaves. Cut olive green ½-inch bias strip 5½ inches long. Following illustration, pin ½-inch bias strip to light blue print 5½×10½-inch rectangle for stem. Cut three 1¼-inch lengths

from olive green ¼-inch bias, and pin to light blue background, tucking ends under ½-inch-wide stem. Stitch stem pieces to background with straight stitch along edges. Fuse sunflower and leaves to light blue background, covering raw edges of bias stems. Fuse sunflower center to sunflower. Using blanket stitch and matching threads, stitch around flower, center, and leaves.

5. Make blocks 2, 4, and 8. Refer to illustration for placement. For block 2, trace and cut out 2 flowers, 2 flower centers, and 3 leaves. Fuse flowers, centers, and leaves to 5½-inch light green print square. For block 4, trace and cut out 2 butterflies. Fuse butterflies to 5½-inch light yellow print square. For block 8, trace and cut out 8 ladybugs. Fuse ladybugs to a 5½-inch green flower print square. Blanket-stitch around edges of flowers, flower centers, leaves, and butterflies with matching threads. Do not stitch around ladybugs.

6. To make block 5, trace and cut out 2 cardinals, 2 beaks, and 2 leaves. Fuse cardinals to remaining 5½-inch green flower print square. Blanket-stitch around edges with matching thread. Fuse cardinal beaks to cardinal bodies. Cut 6-inch strip

from dark green ¼-inch bias, and pin beneath cardinals. Stitch to background with straight stitch along edges. Fuse leaves, and blanket-stitch around edges.

7. To make block 3, trace and cut out 2 flowers, 2 flower centers, and 3 leaves. From dark green ¼-inch bias tape, cut two 1-inch pieces, one 3¼-inch piece, and one 4¼-inch piece. Following illustration, pin ¼-inch bias stems in place on 5½-inch medium blue print square. Stitch to background with straight stitch along edges. Fuse flowers and leaves to background, covering raw edges of stems. Fuse flower centers to flowers. Blanket-stitch around flower and leaf edges, using matching threads.

8. To make block 7, trace and cut out all parts of birdhouse, post, bird, and 6 leaves. Fuse birdhouse pieces, post, and bird to 5½×15½-inch medium blue print rectangle. Blanket-stitch around edges of birdhouse and bird with matching threads. Cut one 15-inch piece from olive green ¼-inch bias tape. Pin in place as vine stem. Stitch to background with straight stitch along edges. Fuse leaves, and blanket-stitch around edges, using slightly contrasting thread.

9. To make block 6, trace and cut out 2 flowers, 2 flower centers, 2 large leaves, and 1 small leaf. From olive green ½-inch bias tape, cut one 4¼-inch piece and one 6¼-inch piece. Pin stems in place on 5½×10½-inch light tan print piece. Fuse leaves to tan background, tucking bottom edges under stems. Blanket-stitch around edges. Stitch stems in place with straight stitch along edges. Do not fuse flowers to background yet.

10. Referring to finished quilt illustration, stitch all blocks together.

11. Fuse flowers and centers in block 6, covering raw edges of stems. Flower on left should overlap seam. Blanket-stitch around edges with matching thread.

12. Cut two 1×45-inch strips from brown print for inner border. Measure quilt vertically through center, and cut 1 strip this length from each 45-inch strip. Stitch to sides of quilt. Measure quilt horizontally through center, and cut remaining strips to this length. Stitch to top and bottom of quilt. Press.

13. Cut three 2½×45-inch strips from light brown print for outer border. Stitch 1 strip to

each side. Cut remaining strip in half, and stitch to top and bottom. Press.

14. Layer quilt front, batting, and back; baste. With white thread, machine-quilt in ditches between blocks and around borders, and outline quilt around shapes. Use black thread to quilt

around ladybugs and to quilt lines defining ladybug wings and heads. Sew beads to cardinal faces for eyes. Sew yellow buttons to block 3 flower centers.

15. Cut three 2½×45-inch dark brown strips for binding. Follow directions on pages 14–15 to stitch binding to quilt.

Dimensions: 21½×26½ inches

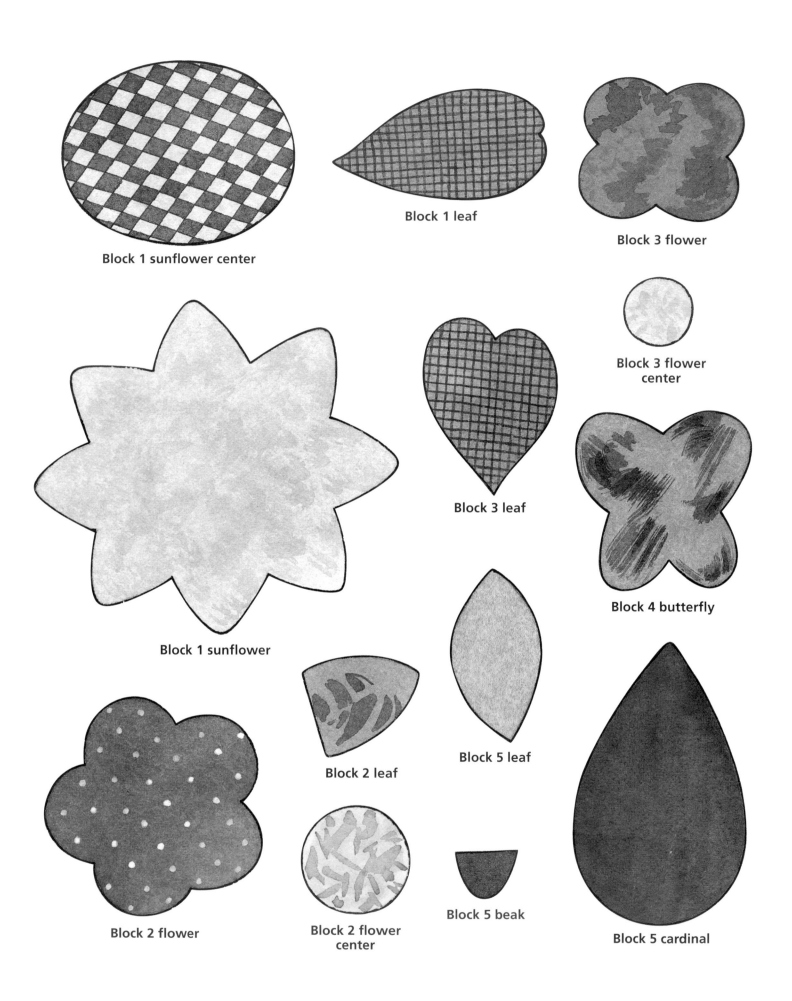

Block 1 sunflower center

Block 1 leaf

Block 3 flower

Block 1 sunflower

Block 3 flower center

Block 3 leaf

Block 4 butterfly

Block 2 flower

Block 2 leaf

Block 5 leaf

Block 2 flower center

Block 5 beak

Block 5 cardinal

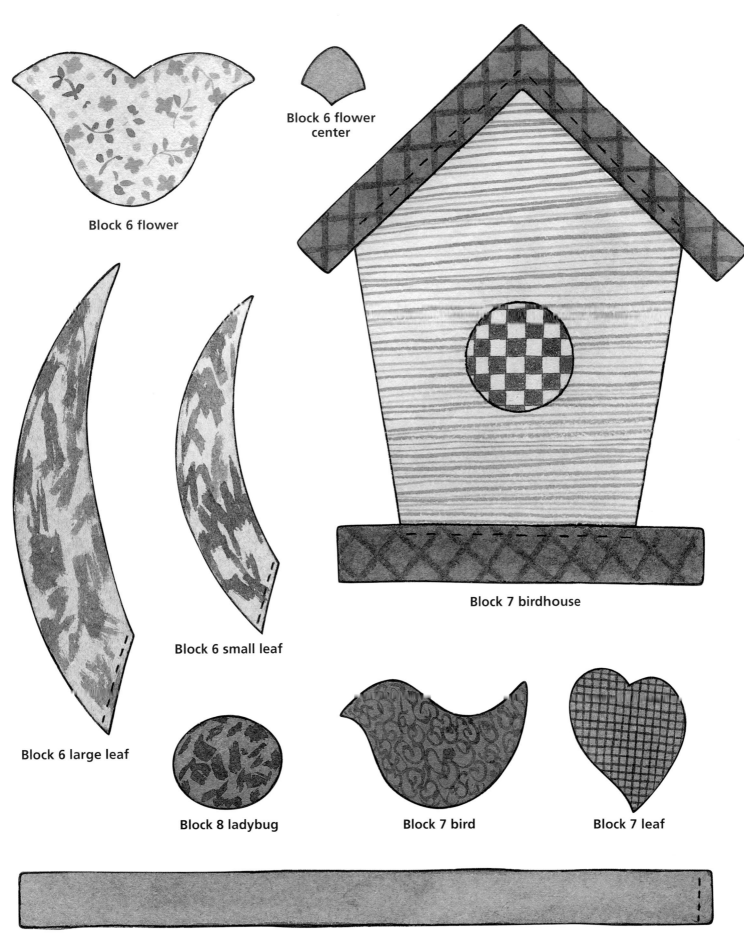

Block 6 flower

Block 6 flower center

Block 6 small leaf

Block 6 large leaf

Block 7 birdhouse

Block 8 ladybug

Block 7 bird

Block 7 leaf

Block 7 post

Mirrored Flower Frame

*Mirror, mirror on the wall—this mirror is the fairest of them all!
Add silk pansies to a plain mirror for a beautiful
addition to your foyer.*

What You'll Need

- Mirror with frame
- Green sheet moss
- Hot glue gun and glue sticks
- 2 yards pansy-print ribbon
- Scissors
- 9 silk pansies
- Assorted small dried flower heads: larkspur, globe amaranth, American statice, ammobium
- Assorted dried fillers: sweet Annie, plumosa, myrtle leaves
- Essential oil (optional)

1. Glue moss over front of frame (some moss can hang over sides).

2. Make 4 small bows out of ribbon, and hot glue a bow in each corner of frame.

3. Glue a silk pansy to center of each bow. Add a pansy on both sides of frame between bows.

4. Glue a pansy to bottom center of frame. At top of frame, glue 1 pansy to the left of center, the other to the right of center.

5. Hot glue remaining assorted dried flowers and fillers on frame. For an extra touch, sprinkle flowers with your favorite essential oil scent.

Spring-Fresh Florals

Brightly colored flowers and tender green leaves will lift your spirits each time you look at this beautiful arrangement.

What You'll Need

- 18- to 20-inch grapevine wreath
- Brown chenille stem
- Hot glue gun and glue sticks
- 3 large red silk tulips with stems
- 2 silk forsythia branches with offshoot branches, one 18 inch and one 12 inch
- Floral wire
- Wire cutters
- 5 silk fern leaves
- Silk ivy trailings
- Ruler
- Silk violet bush with leaves

1. Twist chenille stem on back of wreath to form hook for hanging. Glue in place to secure.

2. Just to the right of the bottom center of wreath, insert 3 tulips at different heights. Glue in place.

3. Insert 18-inch forsythia branch at base of tulip stems, and bend longer stems gracefully up right side of wreath. Use floral wire to hold forsythia in place. Insert shorter forsythia branch at base of tulips, and bend along bottom of wreath, jutting out to left.

4. Glue 3 fern leaves into fan shape to left of tulips. Glue 2 fern leaves to right of tulips, arranging them so they move gracefully up right side of wreath.

5. Cut several ivy trailings into 10- to 12-inch lengths, and glue at base of tulip stems. Allow ivy to hang below wreath.

6. Glue violet bush to wreath where tulips, forsythia, and ferns meet. Bend some leaves up and some down.

Garden Tools and Gloves

With a touch of paint, your tools can be just as flowery as your garden. Even better, these would make a great gift for your favorite gardener!

What You'll Need

- Tracing paper
- Pencil
- Transfer paper
- Garden tools with wood or light-color plastic handles
- Tan garden gloves
- Acrylic paint: green, orange, pink, blue, yellow
- Paintbrushes: 10/0 liner, #2 flat
- Textile medium
- Matte spray varnish

Pattern is 100%.

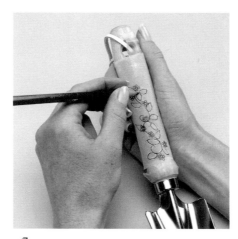

1. Trace and apply flower pattern on handles of tools and tops of gloves.

2. Outline leaves on tools with liner brush and green paint. Fill in leaves with green and #2 flat brush.

3. For gloves only, mix paints with textile medium according to manufacturer's instructions. Line and basecoat leaves with paint mixture.

4. Use end of paintbrush to make 5-dot flowers with orange, pink, and blue paint. Dot the center of each flower with yellow. Let dry.

5. Spray tool handles (not gloves) with matte spray varnish.

Bunny Swag

What could be cuter than these cheerful bunnies hopping along your mantel? Display them during Easter, or use them to decorate your home for the entire spring season!

What You'll Need

- 16-inch small-print fabric squares: green, peach, blue, pink, yellow
- Iron and ironing board
- Tracing paper
- Pencil
- Scissors
- Sewing machine
- White thread
- Ruler
- Fabric scissors
- Fiberfill
- Needle
- 2 plastic rings
- ⅔ yard white gathered lace, ¾ inch wide
- 15-inch lengths satin ribbon, ¼ inch wide: 2 green, 1 peach, 1 blue, 1 pink

Pattern is 100%.

1. Prewash and iron all fabric. Trace and cut out pattern below. Double each fabric piece, with right sides together, and trace pattern on wrong side of fabric. Sew on line with white thread (leave unmarked space for turning). Cut outside of line with scant ¼-inch seam allowance. Clip angles and curves. Turn right side out.

2. Stuff each bunny flat but firm with fiberfill. Slipstitch opening closed.

3. Sew bunnies together nose to tail. Sew plastic rings to back of first and last bunny.

4. Cut five 4-inch lengths of gathered lace. Sew front of lace to back of each ribbon length, allowing extra ribbon for ties. Tie a ribbon around neck of each bunny.

Brightly Blooming Tulips

This springlike pillow will perk up any room. Dimensional appliqués add an interesting twist, and hand-colored sueded cotton fabrics give a soft but vibrant look.

What You'll Need

- ⅜ yard each light blue, dark blue, yellow, red, green, orange sueded cotton
- ½ yard medium blue sueded cotton
- See-through ruler
- Self-healing mat
- Rotary cutter
- Sewing machine
- Quilting needles
- Matching thread
- Iron and ironing board
- Tracing paper
- Pencil
- Scissors
- Fabric scissors
- 2¼ yards cording, ½ inch wide
- Straight pins
- 16-inch polyester fiberfill pillow form

1. From light blue sueded cotton, cut one 12½×18-inch rectangle. Cut one 6½×18-inch rectangle and two 13½×18-inch rectangles from medium blue fabric. Cut two 3×44-inch strips from dark blue. Stitch dark blue strips together end to end, and cut to make 80-inch strip.

2. To make pillow front, stitch light blue rectangle to 6½×18-inch medium blue rectangle along long sides, using ½-inch seam allowance. For pillow back, fold one long edge of one 13½×18-inch medium blue rectangle ¼ inch, and press. Fold over again; stitch. Repeat for other medium blue rectangle. With right sides up, lay dark blue rectangles on flat surface, overlapping finished edges to form 18-inch square. Stay-stitch

across overlapped edges. Set piece aside.

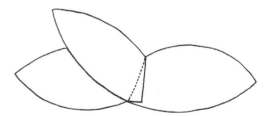

3. Trace and cut out patterns on page 39. Fold yellow and red fabrics in half with right sides together. Trace petal pattern on wrong side of yellow 3 times and on wrong side of red 5 times. Leave at least ½ inch between shapes. Stitch on traced lines all the way around each shape, and cut out, leaving ¼-inch seam allowance. Slash as marked on pattern and turn. Cut 1 yellow and 2 red petals in half. Fold remaining double petals in half along fold line marked on

pattern. Insert half petal in center of each folded petal as shown in illustration on page 36. Stitch to secure at lower cut edge.

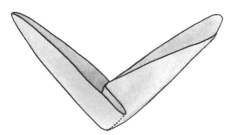

4. Fold green fabric in half with right sides together, and trace leaf pattern 5 times on wrong side. Again, leave at least ½ inch between shapes; stitch along traced lines; and cut out, leaving ¼-inch seam allowance. To shape, fold leaves in half lengthwise with slash to outside as shown above. Press. Fold along fold line. Stitch along lower portion of V shape.

5. Cut two 4×1-inch strips, one 7×1-inch strip, one 6½×1-inch strip, and one 3½×1-inch strip from green fabric. Fold strips in half lengthwise, stitch, and turn.

6. With right sides together, fold orange fabric in half. Trace pot pattern on wrong side of fabric, and stitch all the way around shape on traced line. Cut out, leaving ¼-inch seam allowance. Cut slit, turn, and press. Fold down upper lip of pot

and fold up lower rim along fold lines as shown on pattern, with slit to back. Press.

7. Arrange pot and flowers on pillow top. Cut stems to fit. Place leaves at base of stems along upper lip of pot. Invisibly hand-stitch each shape in place, leaving leaf ends and dimensional parts of pot free.

8. Mark centers of each side of pillow back ½ inch from edge and corners 1 inch from edge. Draw a line to connect marks. This will minimize "rabbit ears" effect.

9. With right sides out, fold dark blue strip over cording, and stitch close to cording using zipper foot. Pin cording along marked line on right side of pillow back, clipping seam allowance of cording at corners to fit. To finish ends of cording, open seams where cording ends meet, cut cording to fit together exactly, overlap seam allowances, and stitch back together to create continuous cording border. Stitch cording to pillow back. With right sides together, pin pillow front and back. Stitch around all 4 sides using zipper foot to get as close to cording as possible. Remove stay-stitching from pillow back, and turn. Insert pillow form.

Dimensions: 17-inch square

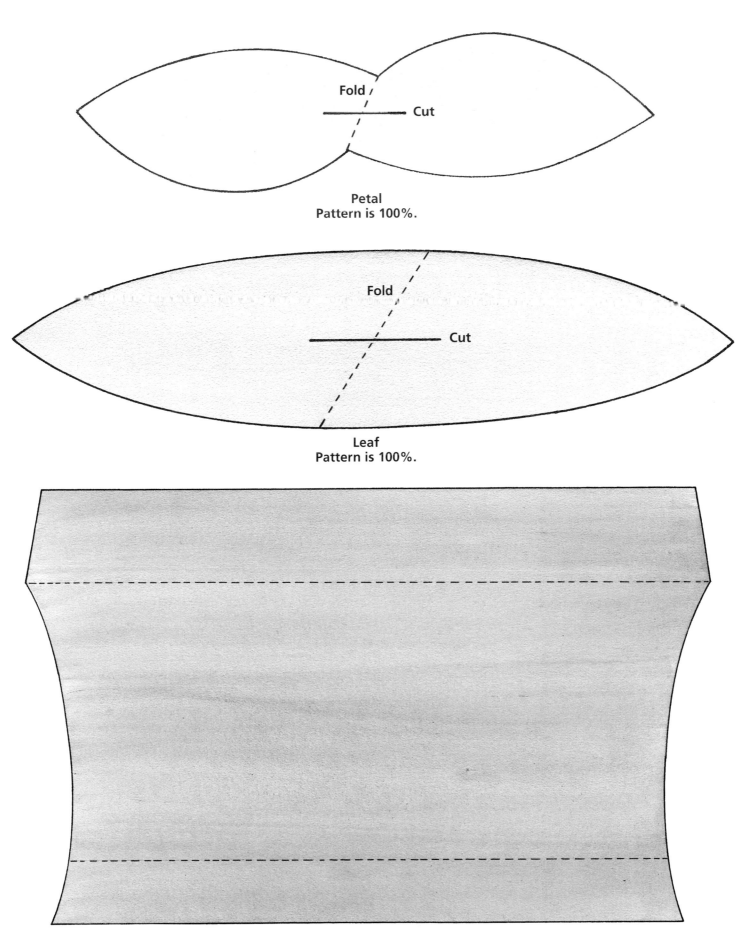

Petal
Pattern is 100%.

Fold

Cut

Leaf
Pattern is 100%.

Fold

Cut

Pot
Enlarge pattern 135%.

Perfectly Pressed Pansies

With these pressed flowers hanging in your window, you'll feel like spring is always just around the corner!

What You'll Need

- 3 pansies
- Fern leaves
- Waxed paper
- Cardboard
- Heavy book
- Two 5×7-inch glass sheets, ⅛-inch thick (have glass shop drill ⅛-inch holes at top corners of glass)
- Glass cleaner
- Lint-free cloth
- Cotton gloves (optional)
- ½-inch-wide adhesive copper foil
- Ruler
- Scissors
- Copper wire: 24 and 14 gauge
- Wire cutters

1. Arrange pansies and ferns on waxed paper, and cover with second sheet of waxed paper. Place cardboard on top, then set between pages of heavy book. Leave book in warm, dry place for 4 to 6 weeks.

2. Lay glass on smooth, dry surface. Clean all sides thoroughly with glass cleaner and lint-free cloth. (Wearing clean cotton gloves will eliminate fingerprints.) Remove flowers and ferns from book and arrange them on sheet of glass; leave border free so foil strips won't cover flowers. Carefully place second sheet of glass on top.

3. Cut strips of copper foil ½ inch longer than sides of glass. Peel off paper backing, and center strip (from front to back of glass) along edge of glass. Press lightly, folding both edges of foil onto glass to adhere. Fold short ends over and around corners. Repeat on all sides.

4. Cut 10-inch length of 24-gauge copper wire. Cut two ½-inch lengths of 14-gauge copper wire for pins.

5. To attach copper hanging wire, insert 10-inch length through both holes in glass from back. Wrap each end of wire tightly around copper pin to anchor wire in place.

Gardener's Delight

This garden wreath is a reminder of the smell of fresh soil, unfolding plants, and the coming of spring. You'll smile every time you see this sunny creation.

What You'll Need

- 18-inch grapevine wreath
- Brown chenille stem
- Hot glue gun and glue sticks
- Ruler
- 12 inches brown twine, ⅛ inch wide
- 2 small sticks, about 1 inch long each
- 6 clay flowerpots: two 1 inch, two 2 inch, two 3 inch
- Floral wire
- Wire cutters
- Silk ivy trailings or other cascading green plant
- 2 small plastic grape clusters
- Small faux bird's nest
- Small faux bird
- Small plastic eggs
- Small bunch white silk flowers
- 2 miniature garden tools
- Sheet moss

1. Twist chenille stem on back of wreath to form hook for hanging. Glue in place.

2. Tie loose knot 4 inches from bottom of twine. Slip a small stick through knot, tighten knot around stick, and thread a 1-inch pot on twine. Make second knot about 4 inches above bottom of flowerpot, insert other stick, tighten knot around stick, and thread other 1-inch flowerpot onto twine. Second pot should overlap top of first pot. Set aside.

3. Glue and wire a 2-inch pot to bottom right of wreath with pot opening facing down and to the right. Glue other 2-inch pot to inside of first pot. Glue and wire a 3-inch pot to the left of 2-inch pots. This pot should be upright. Glue and wire another 3-inch pot above and to the left of first 3-inch pot.

4. Cut several ivy trailings into 10- to 12-inch strands. Glue 3 ivy lengths at base of pots, and angle them up wreath and to the left. Glue in place. Glue 4 ivy pieces under flowerpots, angling them around 2 small flowerpots. Leave a tail or two hanging down.

5. Wire a grape cluster to wreath at 10 o'clock and the other cluster just below pots at base of wreath. Glue bird's nest below 3-inch pots. Glue bird to edge of nest and eggs in nest.

6. Glue short sprigs of ivy into leftmost pot. Glue white flowers into same pot. Angle a garden tool upright in this pot, and glue in place. Place handle of other tool in nest, and glue in place.

7. Tie flowerpots from step 2 to top of wreath. Glue sheet moss to cover any glue or wire.

Spring Garden Sampler

A country cross-stitched sampler will add warmth to any room. Personalize this sampler with your favorite gardening phrase!

What You'll Need

- 16×13 inches misty taupe cross-stitch cloth, 14 count
- #24 tapestry needle
- Embroidery floss (see color chart)

Stitch according to directions in Introduction on pages 15–16. Do all cross-stitch and names on seed packets with 2 strands of floss and all other backstitch with 1 strand.

Colors	DMC#
Light green	368
Medium green	320
Dark green	319
Light yellow	727
Medium yellow	725
Gold	783
Light brown	435
Medium brown	433
Light pink	3713
Medium pink	605
Dark pink	961
Light purple	554
Dark purple	552
Light gray	415
White	000
Wildflowers	(variegated)

Morning Glory Birdhouse

A rustic-looking birdhouse is a charming way to welcome guests to your home!

What You'll Need

- 36×3½-inch stained fence post
- 4×6-inch stained birdhouse
- Ruler
- Hot glue gun and glue sticks
- Hammer and nails (optional)
- 6 stems preserved plumosus fern
- Wire cutters
- 6-foot silk blue morning glory vine garland
- Staple gun and staples
- 6 to 8 stems honeysuckle garland vine
- Sheet moss

1. Hot glue or nail birdhouse 11 inches from top of fence post.

2. Cut and hot glue fern up fence post and around birdhouse.

3. Staple morning glory vine up fence post and around birdhouse, facing flowers in different directions for a more natural look.

4. Glue honeysuckle and moss throughout arrangement.

Daisy Chain Lap Quilt

This cheery lap quilt is a contemporary version of the traditional nine-patch. It's perfect for snuggling up on a cool spring evening or for bringing sunny charm to any room all year round.

What You'll Need

- See-through ruler
- Self-healing mat
- Rotary cutter
- Sewing machine
- Quilting needles
- Matching thread
- Tracing paper
- Pencil
- Scissors
- 1½ yards fusible webbing
- Iron and ironing board
- Fabric scissors
- 17 squares tissue paper, 8×8 inches each
- Straight pins
- 50×65 inches low-loft batting

Quilt fabrics

- 2 yards light blue flower print
- 1½ yards yellow flower print
- 1 yard white-on-white print
- ½ yard each yellow print, green print
- ⅛ yard brown print
- ¼ yard medium blue flower print
- 2 yards backing

Strip set A

Strip set B

1. From light blue flower print, cut eight 3×45-inch strips. Cut seven 3×45-inch strips from yellow flower print. Stitch 1 blue strip to each long side of 3 yellow strips to make 3 A strip sets. Stitch 1 yellow strip to each long side of 2 blue strips. This makes 2 B strip sets.

2. Cut A strip sets into thirty-six 3-inch units. Cut B strip sets into eighteen 3-inch units. Keep A units separate from B units. Stitch 1 A unit to each side of 1 B unit, alternating colors to form a 9-patch. Make eighteen 9-patch squares.

3. From white-on-white print, cut seventeen 8-inch squares. Trace and cut out all pattern pieces on page 51. Iron fusible webbing to wrong side of yellow, green, and brown prints. Trace daisy pattern 17 times on paper side of fusible webbing on yellow print. Trace each leaf pattern 17 times on paper side of fusible webbing on green print. Trace center 17 times on paper side of fusible webbing on brown print. Cut out all pieces, and remove paper backing.

4. Referring to finished quilt photo on page 49, fuse 1 daisy, 1 center, and 2 leaves onto each white-on-white square.

5. Pin square of tissue paper to back of each daisy square. Thread machine with matching thread and light gray thread in bobbin. Using zigzag stitch (2.5W-.5L), stitch around flowers, centers, and leaves. Tear off tissue paper.

6. Stitch blocks together, following finished quilt photo.

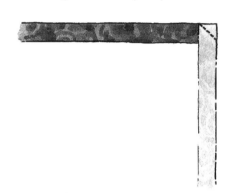

7. From medium blue flower print, cut five 1½×45-inch strips. With right sides together, lay end of 1 strip over end of another strip at right angles. Draw a diagonal line from corner to corner of square formed where strips overlap. Stitch along line, and cut away excess. Open and press. Repeat for other strips to form 1 continuous strip. Measure quilt vertically through center, and cut 2 strips to that length from long strip. Stitch strips to sides of quilt, and press. Measure quilt horizontally through center, and cut 2 strips to that length from long strip. Stitch to top and bottom, and press.

8. From yellow flower print, cut five 3½×45-inch strips. Stitch together to form 1 continuous strip, as in step 7. Measure quilt vertically through center, and cut 2 strips to this length from long strip. Stitch to sides of quilt, and press. Measure quilt horizontally through center, and cut 2 strips to this length from long strip. Stitch to top and bottom, and press.

9. Layer quilt front, batting, and backing; baste. With white thread, quilt in ditches around border and blocks. With blue thread, quilt "X" patterns through 9-patch blocks.

10. From light blue flower print, cut five 2½×45-inch strips. Follow directions on pages 14–15 to stitch binding to quilt.

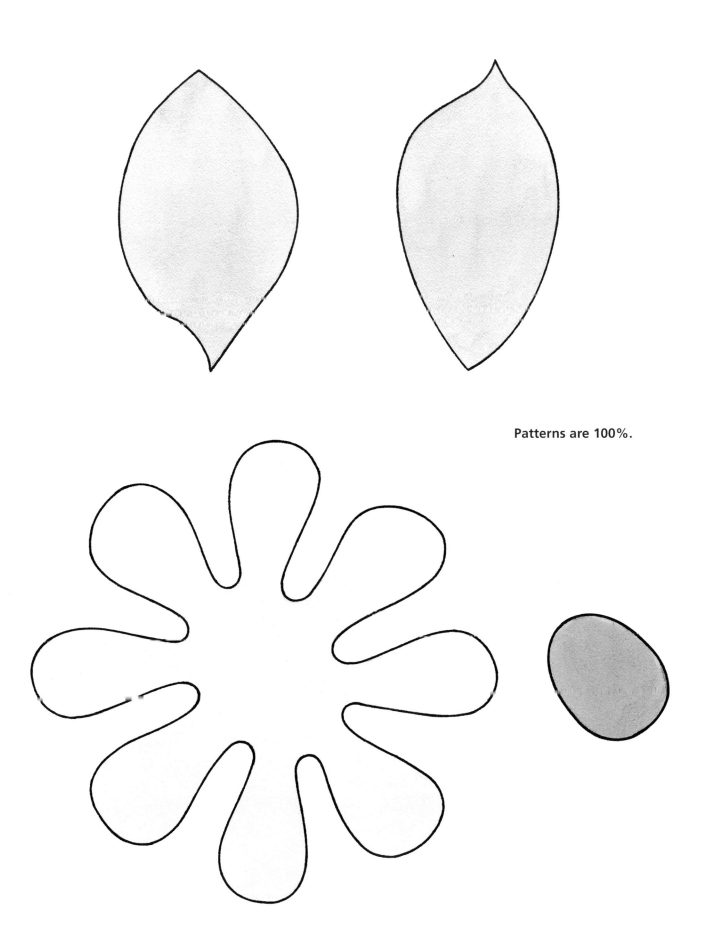

Patterns are 100%.

Brick Doorstop

Welcome everyone into your room with an adorable doorstop made from a simple brick. The flower shop look is sure to be a hit!

What You'll Need

- Brick
- Acrylic paint: cream, red, teal, brown, black, green, yellow, orange
- Paintbrushes: ½-inch flat, four #2 flat, ⅜-inch angle, 10/0 liner
- Tracing paper
- Pencil
- Transfer paper
- Matte spray varnish

1. Wash brick with water. Let dry. Basecoat entire brick with cream and ½-inch flat brush. Let dry. (If brick has a lot of texture, drying time will increase.)

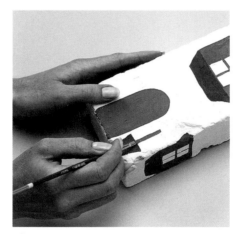

2. Transfer basic pattern on page 54 to brick. Use #2 flat brushes to paint roof, flowerpot, and flower boxes red; door, shutters, and window frames teal; and tree trunk brown. Let dry.

3. Transfer detail pattern to brick (shingles, shutter lines, door dimension, flowerpot, bricks, and leaf placement). Float and line shingles, shutters, tree trunk, door, flower boxes, and flowerpot with black and ⅜-inch angle brush. Also with black, dot doorknob using end of paintbrush. Wash rooftop with water-diluted black.

4. Using water-diluted red, apply faded bricks. Let dry. Using green and #2 flat, apply leaves to flower boxes and tree.

5. Dot flowers on tree and in flower boxes with yellow and orange using end of brush.

6. Use 10/0 liner brush and black to outline "WELCOME" sign. Let dry. Finish with coat of matte spray varnish.

Enlarge pattern 120%.

Try This!

Paint a village of brick houses for a border edging a small garden plot. A few coats of varnish will protect your painting from the elements.

Summer

*Hot days, baseball, newly mown grass, picnics, lemonade—
the many joys of summer! Though the days are long,
summer always seems far too short. Why not prolong it with
decorations to bring the warmth of the sun inside all year long?*

Rustic Rake and Garden Spade

Splendors of your garden are displayed in this colorful mixture of dried flowers, blooming bulbs, and country clay pots.

What You'll Need

- Terra-cotta pots: two 3 inch, one 2 inch
- Acrylic paint: dark green, gold
- 2 small sponges
- 10×27-inch wood rake
- 22-gauge floral wire
- Wire cutters
- Metal garden spade with wood handle
- 3×4×8-inch block dry floral foam
- Craft knife
- Hot glue gun and glue sticks
- Sheet moss
- 3 garden bulbs
- Zinnia seed packet
- 10 to 12 stems fresh or dried pink statice
- Dried purple zinnia head
- 8 stems yarrow
- 10 stems dried poppy pods
- 3 to 4 stems each dried yellow heather, dried green broom
- 5 to 6 stems dried basil lepidium
- 1 or 2 stems fresh or dried lemon leaf (salal)
- 3 to 4 branches honeysuckle garland vine

2. Wire clay pots to center of rake. Wire spade to rake.

3. Use craft knife to cut foam into pieces to fit inside and around clay pots. Glue foam in place. Glue moss to foam.

1. Sponge-paint terra-cotta pots dark green. Let dry. Use other sponge to add gold paint on top of dark green. Let dry.

4. Glue 3 garden bulbs and seed packet in garden space. Cut and glue statice into clay pots. Add remaining dried and fresh flowers in and around clay pots and down handle of rake.

5. Glue honeysuckle vine throughout design.

Lemonade Pitcher and Glasses

Make that summer thirst-quenching treat even more special with hand-painted glasses and a matching pitcher. Lemonade never tasted so good!

What You'll Need

- Clear glass pitcher and tall glasses
- Tracing paper
- Pencil
- Scissors
- Sticky notes
- Ruler
- Overhead projector pen
- Cotton swabs
- Enamel paint: yellow, light yellow, blue
- Brushes: two ¼-inch flat, 2 liner

1. Wash and dry pitcher and glasses. Painting must be done on clean, oil-free surface.

2. Trace and cut out lemon patterns on page 60. For glasses, trace patterns onto sticky notes at sticky edge; cut out. For pitcher, lay lemon patterns on sticky edge of sticky notes, and draw a line around them about ⅛ inch larger than patterns on all sides.

3. Stick lemon, lemon slice, and lemon wedge patterns onto glass surface about 2 inches from bottom (3 inches for pitcher). Draw around patterns with overhead projector pen. Move patterns and repeat. Continue until entire glass has been circled. If there are any stray pen marks on glass inside traced patterns, carefully remove them with slightly damp cotton swab.

4. Using flat brush, fill in lemons with yellow paint. Be careful not to touch traced outline with paintbrush. Use liner brush to paint along curved edge of lemon wedges. For lemon slices, paint circle, then put dot in center and paint 5 spokes radiating out to form lemon segments. Let dry 1 hour before applying second coat of paint.

5. Fill in remaining portions of lemon wedges and slices using liner brush and light yellow paint. Let dry 1 hour, then apply second coat. If more coats of paint are necessary, be sure to let paint dry 1 hour between coats.

7. Use flat brush and blue enamel to paint a checkerboard pattern about ½ inch from bottom of glass. (Use thick layer of glass at bottom as a guideline to keep checkerboard straight, or use overhead projector pen to draw line ½ inch from bottom of glass.) Let paint dry 1 hour between coats.

8. Let paint cure 24 hours. Follow paint manufacturer's instructions for dishwasher-safe finish.

6. Carefully remove pen lines with slightly damp cotton swab.

Patterns are 100%.

Brown Paper Plant Wraps

For an unusual centerpiece or a unique hostess gift, these plant wraps will be the hit of any party!

What You'll Need

- Brown paper
- Pencil
- Ruler
- Scissors
- Pinking shears (optional)
- Plastic storage bag
- Straight pins
- Sewing machine
- Matching thread
- Red felt-tip marker (optional)
- Glue stick
- ½ to 1 yard jute, dyed jute, raffia, ribbon, or fancy cord for each wrap

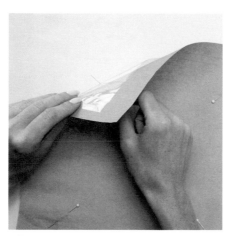

1. Cut 11-inch square out of brown paper (use pinking shears when making green and red wraps). Pin plastic bag to back of paper square. Draw guidelines ½ inch apart from each edge inward. Make 3 more guidelines ½ inch from previous guideline.

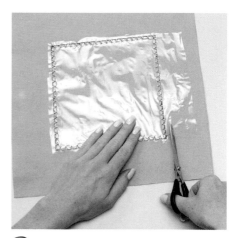

2. Green and red wraps: With sewing machine, secure plastic by using straight stitch and matching thread on innermost guideline.

Orange and blue wraps: Secure plastic by stitching wavy line in matching thread on innermost guidelines.

All wraps: Turn paper over and cut off excess plastic. Though not completely waterproof, this plastic liner will prevent damp flowerpot from spoiling your wrap.

3. *Note: Each line of stitching begins at paper's edge and ends at other edge.*

Green wrap: Using widest satin stitch setting, sew satin stitch on first 2 guidelines and straight stitch on next 2 guidelines. Sew curvy line between 2 straight rows.

Red wrap: Sew wavy line on first row, wide satin stitch on second row, and wide zigzag or loose satin stitch on third row. Sew decorative stitch just inside fourth row and narrow zigzag just inside pinked edge. Use red marker to color from wavy line to outside edge.

Orange wrap: On first row, sew wide yellow satin stitch; on second row, sew orange satin stitch. Stitch orange wavy line on third row.

Blue wrap: As close to cut edge as you can, stitch wide blue satin stitch all around. On first row, sew blue wavy line. Sew wavy line without thread on fourth row. On second row, sew white satin stitch.

4. Pull all threads to back of paper. Glue to secure, then snip ends (never backstitch on paper). Any threads on front can also be glued and trimmed.

5. Cover flowerpots with decorative paper wraps, and secure with jute or other cording.

Tips

Sewing machines are designed to sew on fabric—not paper. Some irregularities are to be expected in your finished product.

- Accept that a small number of skipped stitches will happen. If it happens a lot, replace the needle. A needle that is dull or has a burr on the tip can cause skipped stitches. Also, sewing on paper can fray thread—rethread your machine at the first sign of fray.
- A needle makes a permanent hole in paper. Learn to stop and start with precision. It is helpful to let up on the pedal and hand crank the last few stitches to a critical stopping point.
- Paper can tear easily. If your machine jams thread, don't tug. Cut away all threads in order not to leave a hole in your work.
- Do not set your stitch length too close when making a satin stitch on paper: Needle holes too close together will make a perforated line and tear. (Repairs and/or reinforcements can be made on the back side of your work using tape or a paper patch.)
- Don't worry too much about what will happen to a fancy stitch when you turn a corner. Just sew on the line and try to pivot when the needle is on the right side.
- When you pivot on a corner, make the turn with the needle in the paper. The needle should be on its way up.

Sunflower Garden Wreath

Bright and cheerful silk sunflowers are the focal point of this colorful country garden wreath. Let the warm, sunny tones evoke a cozy feeling in your home.

What You'll Need

- Sunflowers: 3 stems each yellow, rust
- Ruler
- Wire cutters
- 2 stems each yellow silk poppies, chrysanthemums, permanent bittersweet
- 14-inch grapevine wreath
- Hot glue gun and glue sticks

1. Cut sunflower stems to approximately 1 to 2 inches. Cut apart poppy and chrysanthemum stems, and trim individual flower stems to about 5 inches. Cut off all remaining leaves from sunflowers; set aside.

2. Cut bittersweet into separate stems. Insert bittersweet stems into wreath. Wrap and bend stems around wreath.

3. Insert poppies into wreath between bittersweet. Space them evenly around wreath. Repeat with chrysanthemums, leaving open spaces for sunflowers. Glue flower stem ends to secure.

4. Glue heads of yellow sunflowers into wreath. Glue backside of sunflower into wreath. Form triangular pattern with yellow flowers first, then glue 3 rust sunflowers between them. Keep heads of flowers as flat as possible.

5. Glue individual leaves around sunflowers to hide any glue.

Try This!

This wreath can also be used as a candle ring around a glass hurricane. Any variety of country-style silk flowers can be used to complement the sunflowers. The best choices would be flowers that are smaller than sunflowers. For a brighter wreath, use only yellow sunflowers. A bow made of ribbon or raffia can also be added if desired. A country print ribbon, such as gingham, would enhance the wreath's quaint country charm.

Fresh and Fragrant Herb Rack

Add a fresh garden fragrance to your home and have culinary herbs at hand with this eye-catching aromatic herb rack.

What You'll Need

- 3 ounces each dried lavender, dried oregano, preserved mountain mint, dried white larkspur
- 20 stems dried peach roses
- Ruler
- Heavy-duty scissors or wire cutters
- Large wood herb rack with 5 hole openings
- 5 strands raffia

1. Cut dried herbs and flowers 15 to 22 inches long. Make 5 equal bundles of herbs and flowers.

2. Insert 1 bundle through each hole opening in rack. Remove any additional leaves on bottom of stems for easier insertion into opening.

3. Tie each bundle with a strand of raffia.

Try This!

Dry your favorite summer garden herbs for display and cooking, such as dill, rosemary, oregano, mint, parsley, basil, and sage.

Americana Birdhouse

Bring the joy of nature right into your house with this red, white, and blue birdhouse. Now, even on rainy days, you can think about our feathered friends!

What You'll Need

- Medium diamond nest birdhouse
- Fine-grade sandpaper
- Tack cloth
- Paintbrushes: two ½-inch flat, ¼-inch flat, small stencil
- Acrylic paint: cream, red, blue, black
- Painter's tape
- Tracing paper
- Pencil
- Scissors
- Heavy plastic
- Craft knife
- Kemper tool
- Waterbase or acrylic matte spray varnish

1. Sand birdhouse; use tack cloth to remove dust. Use ½-inch paintbrushes to basecoat walls of birdhouse cream and roof and base red. Let dry.

2. To make stripes, tape front and back walls of birdhouse, using same distance between strips as width of tape. With blue

paint and ¼-inch brush, paint stripes. Then line corners up with tape and stripe sides of house. Let dry, and remove tape. Touch up lines with cream, if needed.

3. Trace and cut out stencil pattern on page 69 from heavy plastic. (If you prefer, use store-bought stencil.) Place stencil on

roof, putting a star in opposite corners and 1 star in middle. Using stencil brush, paint stars on roof cream. Move stencil to place stars in remaining corners (be careful not to smear damp paint). Correct any straight lines with red. Let dry.

4. Spatter-paint entire house with Kemper tool and black paint thinned with water. Let dry, and finish with waterbase or acrylic matte spray varnish.

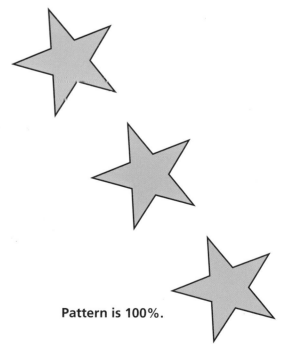

Pattern is 100%.

Antique Watering Can

This elegant watering can makes a charming decorative piece when filled with roses, larkspur, and hydrangeas.

What You'll Need

- Antique watering can
- 3×4×8-inch block dry floral foam
- Craft knife
- Hot glue gun and glue sticks
- Ruler
- Heavy-duty scissors or wire cutters
- 3 ounces each dried white larkspur, dried nigella, dried oregano
- Dried roses: 7 to 8 stems cream, 5 stems dark pink
- Dried hydrangeas: 2 to 3 stems each blue, green

1. Cut and glue foam up to lip of watering can.

2. Cut larkspur, nigella, and oregano 10 to 15 inches long.

Insert bundles of herbs at center of can behind handle, with larkspur in center.

3. Cut dried roses 4 to 8 inches long. Insert cream roses in center in front of handle and dark pink roses at base.

4. Cut hydrangeas 3 to 4 inches long, and insert around edges of container, securing with glue if necessary.

Picket Fence Shelf

Now you can have your own white picket fence—even if you live in an apartment. This shelf is the perfect place to display your prize posies!

What You'll Need

- 2 sections redwood border fencing, 36 inches long
- Safety goggles
- Work gloves
- Crosscut handsaw
- ¾-inch pine board, 6×32 inches
- 2½-inch Phillips-head drywall screws
- Phillips-head screwdriver
- Staple gun and heavy-duty staples
- Variable speed drill and ⅜-inch bit
- Ruler
- Pencil
- Carpenter's wood filler
- Putty knife
- Sandpaper
- White latex satin or semigloss enamel paint
- Paintbrush

1. Place section of border fencing on clean, level work surface. Wearing safety goggles and work gloves, use crosscut handsaw to cut long pickets even with shorter pickets (pickets intended to be inserted in ground). This will be front shelf border.

2. Use 2½-inch drywall screws to attach front shelf border, pickets pointing up, to ¾-inch pine board along lower rail.

3. For back shelf border, carefully remove 2 tall ground-stake pickets. Cut pointed bottom edges straight so all bottom pickets are squared-off. Reposition tall pickets, making sure bottom edges are even with attached pickets. Attach tall pickets to fence brace from back with staples.

4. Mark a point 3 inches down from 2 tall pickets. Drill a counter-sunk hole at this location for attaching shelf to wall.

5. Lay attached fencing facedown on work surface. Attach back section to shelf as you did front section in step 2.

6. Fill in front drywall screws with wood filler, according to package directions. Allow to dry, and sand lightly if necessary.

7. Paint shelf white. Allow to dry overnight. Using drywall screws, attach to wall.

Summer Eucalyptus Wreath

With warm pastels and earthy scents of preserved eucalyptus, hydrangea, and plumosa fern, this wreath is bursting with the colors and smells of summer.

What You'll Need

- Water mister
- 1 pound preserved green jade eucalyptus
- 45 to 50 tips leafless twigs, each 18 inches long
- Ruler
- Garden clippers
- 8-inch round wire wreath form
- Paddle 24-gauge floral wire
- Wire cutters
- 3 inches ribbon, ⅛ inch wide
- 1 bunch each dried dark green plumosa fern, dried baby's breath, dried white gomphrena, dried purple or blue statice
- 10 cream strawflowers
- 1 head seafoam green dried hydrangea, cut in pieces
- Hot glue gun and glue sticks

1. Mist all plants, and cut eucalyptus stems and twigs in varying lengths between 3 and 9 inches.

2. Attach wire by wrapping it once around wreath form and twisting it on back to secure. (Do not cut wire.)

3. Make small bunch of 4 to 6 stems of eucalyptus and 4 or 5 twigs. Place stems of bunch where wire is attached to wreath. Wrap stems 3 times, moving down length of stems with each wrap. At last wrap, you will be ½ inch from end of stems. Make sure wire holds stems snugly but not so tightly that they are crushed.

4. Make another bunch as before. Place this on top of stems of first bunch. As you wrap, first wrap will hold last ½ inch of first bunch as well as top of stems of second bunch. Continue making same size bunches and adding them to wreath. You will need to add about 10 bunches to cover wreath.

5. To add last bunch, cut off end ½ inch of stems. Gently lift first bunch placed on wreath, and slide last bunch under it. Wrap stems of last bunch 3 times to hold it in place. As you wrap, leave second wrap loose enough to pull paddle under so you can tie off and secure wire. Cut wire,

leaving 4-inch tail. Wrap wire around wreath form to secure. Slide wire end under ties and between stems.

6. Cut 4-inch piece of wire for hanger. Wrap it around back of wreath, making loop for hanging. Tie ribbon to hanger so you can find it later.

7. Hang wreath. Glue florals and ferns evenly throughout wreath.

Flower Garden Box

Summer's treasures are intricately executed with garden bunches of dried roses, peonies, and sunflowers divided into geometric patterns and textures.

What You'll Need

- 3×10×18-inch stained wood shadowbox with 8 pockets
- 3 blocks dry floral foam, 3×4×8 inches each
- Craft knife
- Hot glue gun and glue sticks
- 22-gauge floral wire
- Ruler
- Wire cutters
- Sheet moss
- Dried roses: 7 stems each pink, yellow
- 3 stems dried burgundy peonies
- 4 stems dried sunflowers
- 9 stems dried lotus pods (assorted sizes)
- 2 dried pomegranates
- 1 stem dried hydrangea
- 1 package dried linum grass

1. Cut and glue foam into pockets. Cut wire into 3-inch pieces, and shape into U-shape pins.

2. Lightly cover edges of foam with moss; secure with U-shape wire pins.

Try This!

You can use this same technique on any size shadowbox. The garden box can be used as a table arrangement, or make it into a wall hanging by applying a picture hanger to the back. To add spice and fragrance to your garden box, try using cinnamon sticks, garlic bulbs, or bay leaves.

3. Cut dried flowers, and insert into pockets in groups. If necessary, glue to secure.

4. Cover any exposed foam with moss.

Garden Lanterns

*Create a fairyland that will enchant your party-going guests!
These delightful lanterns are a fun project that
the whole family can enjoy.*

What You'll Need

- Tracing paper
- #2 pencil
- Scissors
- Cardboard
- Cream parchment paper
- Pinking shears
- Transfer paper (optional)
- Brush fountain pen (available at art stores)
- Soft eraser
- Art markers: light green, green, orange, fuchsia, red, lime green, chartreuse
- Craft glue
- Strand white mini lights
- Small vinyl-covered paper clips
- Needle and embroidery floss (optional)

1. Trace lantern pattern on page 81 onto cardboard, and cut out. Trace around cardboard template onto parchment paper to make the number of lanterns you'd like to create (3 patterns will fit on an 8½×11-inch sheet of parchment).

2. Cut out patterns from parchment paper, using pinking shears for 2 short sides and long side without circular opening. Use plain scissors to cut remaining long side, carefully cutting out circle. Cut 7 short (about ⅟₁₆ inch) notches around circle.

3. Transfer a design from page 81 to each side of a lantern. (Use transfer paper, or lightly color across design on wrong side with #2 pencil. Then place design, and trace onto shade.) Pull lantern into final round shape, making sure design is positioned well. Transfer remaining designs.

4. Before using brush fountain pen, practice thick and thin lines. Try to keep lines loose and relaxed. Outline all designs on lanterns. Let dry. Gently erase any carbon or pencil marks.

5. Use art markers to fill in designs. Again, be loose—don't follow outlines too closely. Allow color to go outside lines or well within them, sometimes allowing parchment to show through. Color each as follows: leaves light green and green; flowers orange, fuchsia, red, and lime green; butterflies orange, red, chartreuse, and green; watering cans red, orange, chartreuse, fuchsia, and lime green.

6. Apply narrow line of glue to side B only. Work on 1 lantern at a time as glue dries quickly. Carefully bend lantern into curve. Position side A over side B about

¼ inch. When sides are positioned, press together and smooth seam. Repeat for all lanterns.

7. Turn shade upside down. Take a strand of mini lights and, just beneath a light, pinch cord together. Carefully push light through hole in shade until enough cord is exposed on inside of lantern so you will be able to thread a paper clip through a strand of cord. Take care not to damage opening of shade.

8. Gently pull open paper clip so it is spread into a V. Thread clip onto cord.

9. Settle bulb and clip back into neck of lantern, which should be loose but not able to fall off. If necessary, make a stitch with needle and embroidery floss to tighten lantern opening around base of light. Attach remainder of lanterns in same manner. Handle lanterns carefully to prevent dents and creases.

B   A

Patterns are 100%.

Flag Fanfare

Celebrate your love for the United States with an Americana classic—a flag quilt! It truly conveys the pioneer spirit.

What You'll Need

- Self-healing mat
- See-through ruler
- Rotary cutter
- Washable marking pencil
- Sewing machine
- Quilting needle
- White thread
- Fabric scissors
- Iron and ironing board
- 72 various white buttons
- 42-inch square batting
- 1-inch safety pins

Quilt fabrics

- ⅝ yard red
- 1⅔ yards white
- ¾ yard blue
- ½ yard black
- 1½ yards backing
- ½ yard binding

1. For center star section, cut 20 red 2-inch squares and 16 white 3½×2-inch rectangles. Use marking pencil to draw diagonal line corner to corner on wrong side of 16 red squares.

2. (Unless otherwise noted, all seam allowances are ¼ inch and all pieces are matched right sides together. After sewing, press all seams to darkest fabric.) Lay 2-inch red diagonal-marked square on right side of 3½×2-inch white rectangle. Sew along diagonal, and trim fabric ½ inch away from seam line. Repeat with remaining diagonal-marked red squares and white rectangles.

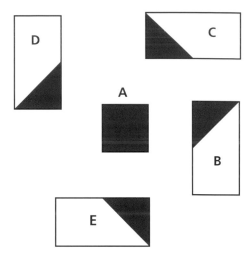

3. Following diagram above, sew piece A to top of B. Sew piece C to top of AB. Sew piece E to bottom left of piece B and bottom of A. Sew piece D to top left of piece E and left of piece AC. Sew 4 star blocks together to make large block.

4. For flag, cut 4 white 2×18½-inch strips, 8 red 2×18½-inch strips, 8 white 2×9½-inch strips, 4 red 2×9½-inch strips, and 4 blue 9½×5-inch rectangles.

5. Sew together white, red, and white 2×9½-inch strips. Repeat with remaining 2×9½-inch strips (you should end up with 4 sets). Sew each set to right side of blue 9½×5-inch rectangle (piece A). Sew together red, white, and red 2×18½-inch strip. Repeat with remaining 2×18½-inch strips (you should end up with 4 sets). Sew each set to bottom of piece A to create flag. Sew buttons to blue section of flag. Sew flags around center stars block.

6. For accent border, cut 4 black 1½-inch strips selvage to selvage. Measure through center vertically of flags block, and cut 2 strips this measurement. Sew strips to sides of flags block. Measure through center horizontally, and cut 2 strips this measurement. Sew strips to top and bottom of block.

7. For bear paws corners, cut 20 white 2½-inch squares, 12 white 2⅞-inch squares (cut in half diagonally), 16 white 4½-inch squares, 4 white 4⅞-inch squares (cut in half diagonally), 4 white 9×12-inch rectangles, and 4 blue 9×12-inch rectangles.

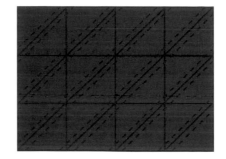

8. To make speedy triangles, place white and blue 9×12-inch rectangle right sides together. Draw grid on rectangle of twelve 2⅞-inch squares. Draw diagonal line through each corner of every square. Sew ¼ inch away from diagonal line, on both sides of line. Cut on all drawn lines (see diagram above). Repeat with remaining rectangles.

9. Assemble 12 bear paw sets according to Diagram A. Assemble 8 bear paw sets according to Diagram B. Assemble 4 bear paw sets according to Diagram C.

10. Assemble 4 corners according to finished photo. When joining, right sides are even. Add corners onto center flags block. Put opposite corners on first (top and bottom) and then remaining 2 corners.

11. Cut backing and batting 2 inches larger than quilt face. Place quilt face on top of backing and batting. Pin baste with 1-inch safety pins. Mark quilting design with washable marking pencil. Starting in center, quilt with small even stitches. Trim batting and backing even with quilt face.

12. Cut six 2½-inch-wide strips for binding. Follow directions on pages 14–15 to stitch binding to quilt.

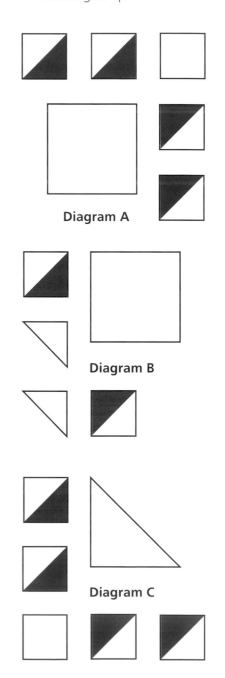

Diagram A

Diagram B

Diagram C

Fall

The crisp, cool autumn air and the crunch of fallen leaves evoke memories of going back to school, Halloween dress-up, and family gatherings. Bring the reds, yellows, oranges, and browns of autumn into your home with these simple but inventive crafts.

Copper Plant Markers

These decorative plant markers will add charm to your garden while helping you remember where you planted your vegetables!

What You'll Need

- 3 wood pieces, 3⅝×5⁷⁄₁₆ inches each
- Wood sealer
- Paintbrushes: three ¾-inch flat, #1 liner, #4 round
- 3 paint stirring sticks
- Dark green acrylic paint
- Gloss paint: bright green, silver, black, white, yellow, red, orange
- Tracing paper
- Pencil (with good eraser)
- Ruler
- 3 pieces tooling copper, 3⅝×5⁷⁄₁₆ inches each
- 0000 steel wool
- Newspaper
- Stylus
- Cotton balls
- Clear silicone glue
- 12 bronze thumbtacks
- Small hammer
- Paper towels

1. Seal wood with wood sealer and ¾-inch flat brush. Let dry. Basecoat paint sticks with dark green and flat brush. When dry, paint 1 or 2 coats of bright green using flat brush.

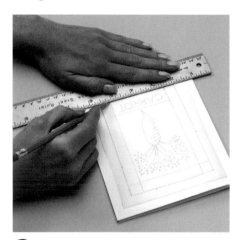

2. Copy patterns on page 89 onto tracing paper; add ½-inch borders. Extend outside design lines to edges, making square in each corner.

3. Gently rub fronts and backs of copper with steel wool. Fold newspaper several thicknesses. Place pattern on top of copper, and place on newspaper. Imprint design with stylus, including border lines. Remove pattern.

 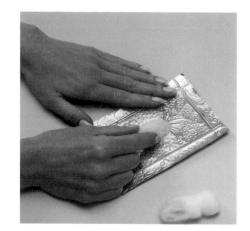 

4. Turn copper over. To make imprint more pronounced, trace on both sides of all lines and dots of design with stylus. Add scribble lines along border with stylus. Shape roots and radish and onion tops by pressing with pencil eraser. Turn to front. With stylus, press dots in background around vegetables.

5. Glue cotton to backs of root sections to keep them rounded. Apply glue to one side of wood pieces, and place copper on top. With small hammer, pound a thumbtack in each corner in front. If copper has stretched, bend excess copper over edge.

6. Using liner brush for smaller areas and round brush for other areas, paint plant markers. Use silver along borders and around letters, keeping paint very wet. When borders are tacky, pat with paper towel to remove some silver. Paint dotted background black.

7. Paint vegetable tops bright green. While still wet, add white and touches of yellow, and blend along carrot and radish stems, on midsection of onion, and on a few onion tops. Paint onion root white. Blend red and yellow along edges. Paint radish red, and highlight with white. Paint carrot root orange, and blend red along left side and white on root tip. Highlight with white. Paint border stripes and lettering bright green. Let dry.

8. Glue painted stirring sticks to back, aligning top edges.

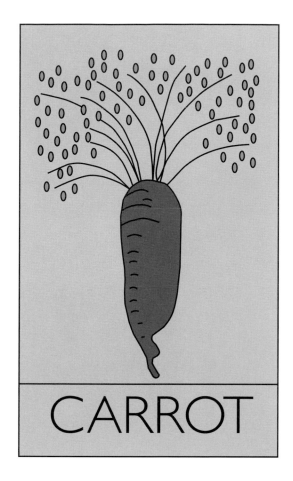

CARROT

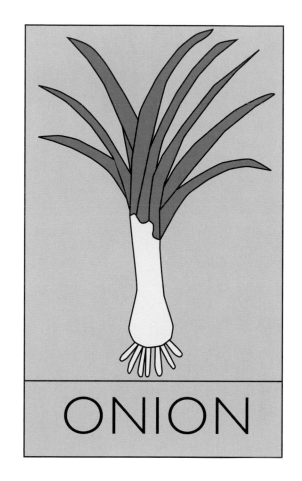

ONION

RADISH

Patterns are 100%.

Gilded Harvest

A fall wreath of classic eucalyptus is given a regal update with gold gilding. Lush, deep-tone hydrangeas and harvest berry clusters add texture and interest to the rich golden highlights.

What You'll Need

- 24-inch premade eucalyptus wreath (dried, plastic, or silk)
- Gold spray paint
- 7 red silk hydrangea stems
- 5 berry stems
- Ruler
- Wire cutters
- Hot glue gun and glue sticks
- 8 small bunches caspia or statice (dried or silk)

1. Apply gold spray paint to wreath. Spray evenly to coat all branches. Let dry overnight.

Tip

If you can't find a eucalyptus wreath, wire 5 to 6 stems of eucalyptus into a bunch with floral wire. Each bunch should be 7 to 8 inches long. Make enough bunches to cover the wire frame. Wire eucalyptus bunches to the frame with small pieces of floral wire. Keep all bunches going in the same direction.

2. Cut stems of hydrangea and berries 1 to 2 inches long. Glue stems into eucalyptus, alternating hydrangea and berry clusters and following direction of eucalyptus.

3. Glue in pieces of caspia or statice between hydrangeas and berries.

Try This!

- Add extra highlights by tucking in silk or dried fall leaves. For an extra gilded touch, lightly spray leaves with gold paint. (Remember to let spray-painted materials dry overnight.)
- Any type of silk or dried fluffy filler material can be used in place of caspia or statice. Choose materials smaller than the larger hydrangea and berry clusters, which should appear dominant. The trick is to pick materials with different textures so they contrast nicely.

Down-Home Veggie Wall Hangings

Give your kitchen a warm country touch with these adorable wall hangings. Each quilt can be made with fabric scraps and buttons from your sewing basket.

What You'll Need

All quilts

- See-through ruler
- Self-healing mat
- Rotary cutter
- Washable marking pencil
- Sewing machine
- Quilting needles
- Matching thread
- Scissors
- Iron and ironing board
- ⅛ yard each or scraps 8 different fabrics for borders (colors should harmonize with central block)
- 8 buttons, assorted colors and sizes
- Jute
- 9×12 inches each backing fabric and low-loft batting
- ¼ yard binding fabric

Eggplant

- Tracing paper
- ⅛ yard each cream print, purple print, dark green print

Onion

- ⅛ yard each cream print, yellow print, medium green print

Carrot

- ⅛ yard each tan print, orange print, green-and-cream print

Radish

- Tracing paper
- ⅛ yard each tan print, red print, white-on-white print, dark green print

You will use template-free angle piecing and bias rectangle techniques to make the Down-Home Veggie Wall Hangings.

TEMPLATE-FREE ANGLE PIECING

To add a square, draw diagonal line from corner to corner on wrong side of fabric square. Following diagram, lay square on other fabric piece with right sides together. Stitch on diagonal line, and cut away ¼ inch from seam on outer side. Press open. To add second square, repeat steps but with diagonal line going in opposite direction.

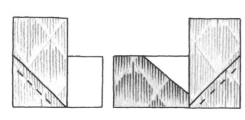

To add a larger piece, lay fabric pieces with right sides together as shown in diagram. Draw diagonal line from corner to corner of square formed where top fabric covers bottom fabric. Stitch on line, cut away ¼ inch from seam, and press open. To add second piece, repeat steps as shown in diagram.

BIAS RECTANGLES

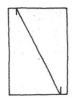

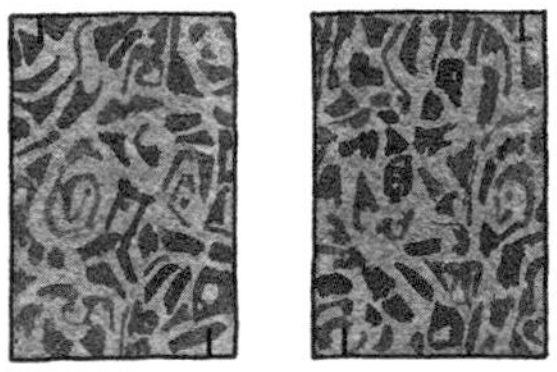

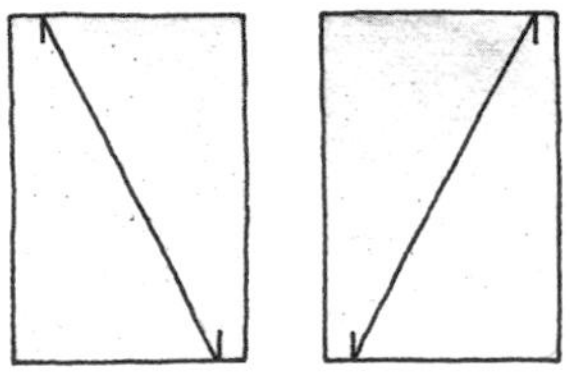

1. Cut equal-size rectangles of background fabric and contrast fabric. On right side of background fabric, mark ⅛ inch in from outside edges at top and bottom. On wrong side of

contrasting fabric, mark ⅛ inch in from outside edges at top and bottom. Note that marks are opposite for right and left bias rectangles. On wrong side of contrast pieces only, draw diagonal line linking ⅛-inch marks.

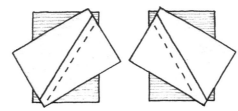

2. With right sides together, place contrast fabric on top of background fabric. For right bias rectangle, turn contrast rectangle counterclockwise until upper right corner is within ⅛ inch of upper left corner of background rectangle and lower left corner is within ⅛ inch of lower right corner of background. For left bias rectangle, turn contrast rectangle clockwise until upper left corner is within ⅛ inch of upper right corner of background and lower right corner is within ⅛ inch of lower left corner of background.

3. Stitch on line. Cut away excess, leaving ¼-inch seam allowance. (See dotted lines in step 2 diagram.) Open and press.

If making more than 1 bias rectangle, use chain piecing technique described on page 10.

BORDERS

Follow these general directions to make borders for the Down-Home Veggie Wall Hangings. Each border strip is cut from a different fabric. All corner squares for 1 quilt are the same color.

1. From fabric scraps, cut two 1¼×8-inch strips (inner sides); two 1¼×5½-inch strips (inner top and bottom); two 1¼×9½-inch strips (outer sides); two 1¼×7-inch strips (outer top and bottom); and eight 1¼-inch squares. For binding cut one 2½×44-inch strip. Cut this strip into two 2½×11-inch strips for sides and two 2½×9½-inch strips for top and bottom.

2. Stitch 1 corner square to each end of all top and bottom strips (1¼×5½-inch strips and 1¼×7-inch strips).

3. To finished vegetable block, stitch 1¼×8-inch inner side strips, then 1¼×5½-inch top and bottom strips (with corner squares). Add 1¼×9½-inch outer side strips, then 1¼×7-inch outer top and bottom strips with corner squares.

4. Sew buttons on each corner square with jute. Knot jute on top side.

5. Quilt as desired (wall hangings shown are hand-quilted; to save time or create a slightly different look, machine-quilt designs).

6. Follow directions on pages 14–15 to stitch binding to quilt.

LEAVES AND TOPS

1. For each leaf or top, trace pattern piece on page 98 on wrong side of fabric; cut out. Turn pattern over, trace, and cut out reversed shape. Each pattern has line showing where to cut slit for turning. Cut slit in 1 piece only.

2. With right sides together, stitch matching leaf and top pieces together. Use ⅛-inch seam allowance and smaller stitches. When sewing points, it's easier to turn and get a smooth point if you stitch 1 stitch across point. Trim all points, and clip into corners.

3. Turn through slit opening on back (it's not necessary to close opening since it will be on back side). Press. If desired, use white thread to hand-stitch lines to represent leaf veins.

4. With slit to back, hand-stitch tops and leaves to vegetable blocks with dark green thread.

EGGPLANT

Dimensions: 8½×11 inches

1. From cream print, cut one 1¾×18-inch strip and one 5½×2¾-inch rectangle. Cut strip into two 1¾-inch squares, one 1½×3-inch rectangle, one 1½×2-inch rectangle, two 1×3¼-inch rectangles, one 1×1½-inch rectangle, and two 1-inch squares. From purple print, cut one 3½×18-inch strip. Cut strip into one 3½×2-inch piece, one 3¼×4½-inch piece, and one 1½×4-inch piece.

2. Stitch 3½×2-inch purple piece to 1½×2-inch cream piece along 2-inch sides. Using template-free angle piecing, stitch 1-inch cream square to upper right corner of 1½×4-inch purple

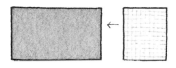
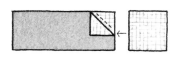

piece. Add 1×1½-inch cream piece to right side. Join units and add 1½×3-inch cream piece to left side.

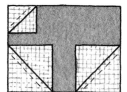

3. Using template-free angle piecing technique, stitch 1¾-inch cream squares to bottom corners of 3¼×4½-inch purple piece. Stitch 1-inch cream square to upper left corner of purple piece. Add one 1×3¼-inch cream piece to each side.

4. Assemble eggplant, adding 5½×2¾ inch cream piece to top.

5. Add borders, following directions on pages 94–95.

6. Use directions for leaves and tops to make eggplant top from dark green print.

7. Layer front, batting, and back; baste. With white thread, hand-quilt in ditches around center block and between inner and outer borders. Hand-quilt lines in eggplant and diagonal grid pattern in background.

8. Follow directions on pages 14–15 to stitch binding to quilt.

ONION

Dimensions: 8½×11 inches

1. From cream print, cut one 4½×44-inch strip. Cut strip into one 4½×5½-inch rectangle, one 4×2-inch rectangle, one 4×1¾-inch rectangle, one 2¾×1¼-inch rectangle, two 1½-inch squares, and two 1-inch squares. From yellow print, cut one 2¾×3¼-inch rectangle. From medium green print, cut one 1¼×44-inch strip.

 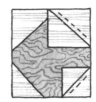

2. Lay yellow rectangle right side up with short sides at top and bottom. Using template-free angle piecing technique, stitch 1½-inch cream square to upper left corner of yellow and 1-inch cream square to lower left corner. Open and press. Repeat for right side of yellow rectangle.

3. Fold green strip in half lengthwise with wrong side out and stitch. Turn. Cut into one 6½-inch strip, two 5½-inch strips, one 5-inch strip, and one 4½-inch strip. Tie knot at one end of each strip.

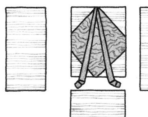

4. Lay 2 green strips on top of onion unit with knotted ends out and unknotted ends at upper

corner of onion. Stitch 4½×5½-inch cream piece to top of onion unit, including unknotted ends of green strips in seam. Stitch 2¾×1¼-inch cream piece to bottom of yellow. Stitch 4×2-inch cream piece to left side of yellow and 4×1¾-inch cream piece to right side of yellow.

5. Hand-stitch remaining onion tops to quilt with unknotted ends behind 2 tops already sewn in. Fold all sewn tops up and stitch over ends of tops just added. Do not stitch knotted ends to background yet.

6. Repeat steps 5 and 7 of eggplant. Hand-quilt lines of onion. Repeat step 8 of eggplant.

7. Hand-stitch knotted ends of onion to quilt. Cut eight 5-inch lengths of jute, and tie knot in center of lengths. Hand-stitch knot to bottom of onion, allowing ends to hang down to form roots. Trim ends.

CARROT

Dimensions: 8½×11 inches

1. From tan print, cut one 1¾×44-inch strip and one 5½×2¼-inch rectangle. Cut strip into two 1¾×1½-inch rectangles, four 1¾×4¾-inch strips, two 1-inch squares, and one 1×5½-inch strip. From orange print, cut one 1¾×22-inch strip. Cut strip into two 1¾×4¾-inch pieces and one 3×1½-inch piece. From green-and-cream print, cut one ¾×44-inch strip.

2. Using template-free angle piecing technique, stitch two 1-inch tan squares to upper corners of 3×1½-inch orange piece. Stitch one 1¾×1½-inch tan piece to each side of unit.

3. Make 1 right and 1 left bias rectangle using 1¾×4¾-inch tan and orange pieces. Stitch together with orange on the

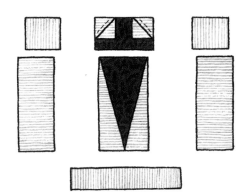

inside, and add one 1¾×4¾-inch tan piece to each side of unit. Stitch 1×5½-inch tan strip to bottom. Stitch upper and lower parts of carrot together.

4. For carrot top, cut green strip into 4-, 5-, and 6-inch lengths. Fray edges. Gather random lengths together with ends even, and twist ends together. You don't have to use all carrot top pieces.

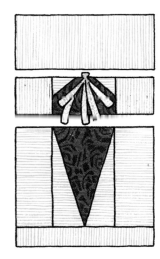

5. Lay twisted ends of carrot tops at top of carrot unit in center of carrot. Stitch 5½×2¼-

inch tan piece to top of carrot, including carrot top in seam. Flip up carrot top pieces and hand-stitch to quilt about 1 inch above orange. Carrot top will extend over borders.

6. Repeat steps 5 and 7 of eggplant. Hand-quilt curved lines in carrot and grid pattern in background. Repeat step 8 of eggplant.

RADISH

Dimensions: 8½×11 inches

1. From tan print, cut one 3½×44-inch strip. Cut strip into two 3½×1¼-inch strips, one 3×5½-inch rectangle, two 3×1¾-inch rectangles, two 1¾-inch squares, one 1¼×5½-inch strip, and two 1-inch squares. From red print, cut one 4×3½-inch rectangle. From white-on-white print, cut one 3×1¾-inch rectangle. From dark green print, cut pieces to make 2 small leaves and 1 large leaf, following directions on page 95.

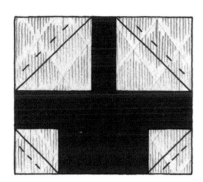

2. Using template-free angle piecing, stitch two 1¾-inch tan squares to upper corners of red and two 1-inch tan squares to lower corners of red. Add one 3½×1¼-inch tan piece to each side of unit.

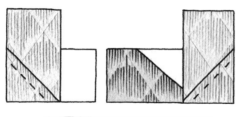

3. Using template-free angle piecing technique, stitch 3×1¾-inch tan pieces to white. Stitch radish unit to root unit. Press. Stitch 3×5½-inch tan piece to top of radish.

4. For root, cut 2½-inch length of jute, and tie knot in one end. Lay jute over root unit with unknotted end at point of root. Stitch 1¼×5½-inch tan piece to bottom of root unit, including unknotted end of jute in seam.

5. Make leaves, following directions on page 95. Using dark green thread, hand-stitch to top of radish as shown.

6. Repeat steps 5 and 7 of eggplant. Hand-quilt curved lines in radish. Repeat step 8 of eggplant.

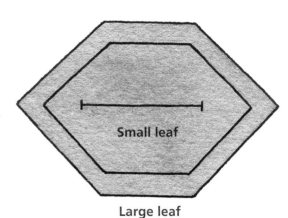

Small leaf

Large leaf

Enlarge patterns 110%.

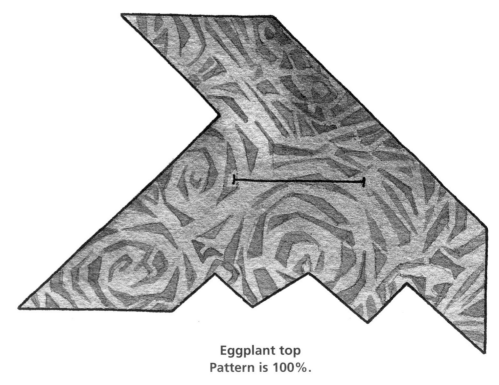

Eggplant top
Pattern is 100%.

Halloween Delights

Perfect for holding Halloween goodies, this special, sturdy bag is simple to make and will last for years to come.

What You'll Need

- ¾ yard ultra-hold fusible webbing
- Tape measure
- Pencil
- Fabric scissors
- 7 coordinating Halloween prints
- Iron and ironing board
- 17×12-inch brown paper bag with handles
- Scrap black fabric
- Tracing paper
- Scissors
- Permanent black marker
- 2 yards fusible vinyl

1. Cut two 17×12-inch pieces of fusible webbing. From Halloween prints, cut 12×5-inch piece, 4⅛×7-inch piece, 8×7-inch piece, and 5×12-inch piece. Also cut 17×12-inch piece for back of bag.

2. Lay fabric sections for bag front onto piece of fusible webbing, and fuse according to manufacturer's directions. Adhere fabric for back of bag to other piece of fusible webbing. Remove paper backing. Bond to front and back of bag.

3. Iron fusible webbing to remaining fabric for cutouts. Trace and cut out patterns on page 100. Then trace patterns on desired fabrics; cut out. Remove paper backing.

4. Arrange cutouts on bag front using photo as guide. Press in place. Write "Trick or Treat" on moon with permanent marker.

5. Cover entire bag with vinyl. To determine amount, measure bag beginning at top of bag front, down under bag bottom, and back up to top of bag back. Add 1 inch to this measurement, and cut out.

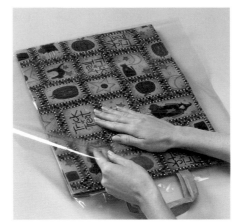

6. Center bag bottom on center of paper side of vinyl. Vinyl will be wider than bag (excess will help to cover bag sides). Mark bag bottom corners on paper backing. Cut vinyl to mark from each edge.

7. Remove paper backing to first set of cuts. Lay bag front onto sticky side of vinyl. Hand-press in place. Fold excess vinyl onto sides of bag. Continue to remove paper backing to next set of cuts. Hand-press bag bottom

in place, leaving excess on sides only. Remove remaining paper backing, hand-press to bag back, and fold excess to bag sides. Fold bottom excess up onto bag sides. Fold any excess at top of bag to inside, making cuts at handles for proper fit. Iron according to manufacturer's directions. Cut pieces of vinyl to fit uncovered bag area on sides. Bond using manufacturer's directions.

Enlarge patterns 110%.

Earthy Autumn Swag

Faux mushrooms and gourds seem to magically sprout among moss, dried fall leaves, and pinecones on a bundle of natural birch branches. Bittersweet vines add rich fall color and texture to this easy-to-make swag.

What You'll Need

- 24-gauge floral wire
- Brown floral tape
- Birch branches
- Ruler
- 2 stems bittersweet (artificial or dried)
- Hot glue gun and glue sticks
- 3 artificial mushrooms
- 2 artificial gourds
- 3 assorted pinecones
- Dried or silk fall leaves
- Natural green sheet moss

1. Wrap floral wire with brown floral tape. Making sure all branches are going in the same direction, tightly tie bundle of birch branches together with taped wire about 3 inches from top of bundle. Form hook with wire on back of branches so they hang vertically.

2. Wire bittersweet vines to sides of bundle. Place 1 stem on right and 1 stem on left of bundle. Make sure stems of bittersweet are tied into bundle so bittersweet hangs vertically.

3. Glue mushrooms, gourds, and pinecones to birch bundle. Glue in leaves and pieces of moss to hold materials in place as well as to hide glue and wire.

4. Bend bittersweet branches up and over cluster of mushrooms and gourds for movement.

Try This!

- The long, low shape of this swag lends itself perfectly for the center of a table. Add taper candles and a few votives for an extra-warm glow.

- For more color, glue small silk or dried fall flowers into the swag. Or add miniature faux pumpkins for even more fall flair!

Autumn Berry Candle Rings

Warm a cool fall evening with these cozy candle rings. Perfect as a table centerpiece, the berry rings can also hang on a door as a colorful and bright holiday wreath.

What You'll Need

- 24-gauge floral wire
- Brown or dark green floral tape
- Ruler
- Wire cutters
- 8 stems orange berry sprays with leaves
- 3 pillar candles, two 3×6 inches and one 6×6 inches

Tip
These delightful candle rings are perfect around all different sizes of candles. They can even be used around glass hurricanes. The size of the candle will determine the size of the ring you will need.

1. Wrap floral wire with floral tape. Twist tape tightly around wire, and cut wire into 6-inch pieces.

2. Choose berry stems that have sprays of berries instead of clusters. Spray portion should be at least 8 to 12 inches long. Cut off stem end of sprays.

3. Using pieces of taped floral wire, wire 2 berry sprays together. Tie berry sprays together as tightly as possible, then form them around a 3×6-inch candle by bending into a ring. Wire 6 to 8 places around ring to hold securely.

4. Bend berries to form a flat side where berries touch the candle so ring sits evenly. Keep berries going in same direction. Repeat for second small ring.

Tip
Keep the ring as tight and full of berries as possible. Some berry sprays are available with tiny leaves and stems. Others are just berries. Experiment with different types of sprays. When tiny berries are grouped together, they create a cozy glow for fall entertaining.

5. Repeat process with remaining sprays around larger candle. Wire in as many extra berries as needed to get full, round shape. Place larger candle ring in center of table, with smaller candle rings on either side.

Country Apple Basket

*A-tisket, a-tasket, a country apple basket!
And it's just the right size for carrying everything from
apples to craft supplies.*

What You'll Need

- Woven basket
- Paintbrushes: two 1-inch flat, six #4 round, two #10 flat, #0 liner
- Dark walnut stain
- Paper towels
- Acrylic paint: red, cream, peach, brown, green
- Brown paper bag
- Pencil
- Tracing paper
- Transfer paper
- Stylus
- Spray varnish

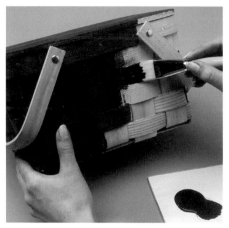

1. Basket should be smooth and free of dust. Stain basket and lid using a 1-inch flat brush and dark walnut stain. Wipe off excess stain with paper towel. Use other 1-inch flat brush to paint top of handles red. When dry, "sand" lid with piece of brown paper bag.

2. Transfer pattern on page 108 to lid top. Use #4 round brush to fill in large apple and edges of other 2 apples with red. Use other round brushes to fill in lightest areas with cream and remaining areas with peach. Paint seeds brown.

3. Double load a #10 flat brush with red and peach. With peach side out, paint highlight on edges of apples. Fill in solid highlight with peach (upper right side of large apple).

5. Fill in flower petals with cream. Fill in flower center with peach. Double load round brush with red and peach to shade the center. Use #0 liner to paint thin lines around and inside petals.

6. Double load a #4 round brush with green and cream to fill in leaves and stems.

7. Use end of brush dipped in cream to make dots in clusters of 3. You may also add dots on basket, staggering groups of dots in middle 2 rows of weaving (see finished photo). Let dry, then spray with 2 to 3 coats of varnish.

4. Double load a #4 brush with brown and peach to fill in stems. Use peach to fill in top circle of stems.

Enlarge pattern 120%.

Country Scents Quilt

What better way to bring the country into your kitchen than with chickens, apple pie, jam, and tea?

What You'll Need

- See-through ruler
- Self-healing mat
- Rotary cutter
- Sewing machine
- Quilting needle
- Matching thread
- 27-inch square batting
- Safety pins
- Iron and ironing board
- ⅜ yard fusible webbing
- Tracing paper
- Pencil
- Scissors
- Fabric scissors
- Washable marking pencil

Quilt fabrics

- ½ yard background
- ⅜ yard each lattice, binding
- Scraps: light and dark colors, multicolor prints
- ¼ yard accent border
- ⅜ yard outside border
- ¾ yard backing

Appliqué fabrics

- 5-inch squares for chickens
- 9-inch square for pie
- 6-inch square for teapot
- 5-inch square for basket
- 3-inch square for each apple
- 3-inch square for jam jar

Tips

- All seam allowances are ¼ inch.
- Always iron seams to darkest fabric.
- Measurements are listed widths first, then heights.

1. Section 1: Cut 5½×4-inch rectangle from background fabric and 1½×6-inch strip from lattice. To make checkerboard, cut five 1½-inch squares from dark-colored fabric scraps and five 1½-inch squares from light-colored scraps. Sew 5 alternating light to dark squares together right to left. Sew 5 alternating dark to light squares together right to left. Sew strips on top of each other with darker outside squares on top. Sew checkerboard to top of 5½×4-inch background piece. Sew 1½×6-inch lattice piece to right side of checkerboard/ background block.

2. Section 2: Cut 10½×6-inch rectangle from background fabric and 1½×6-inch strip and 17½×1½-inch strip from lattice. Sew 10½×6-inch background piece to right side of block from Step 1. Sew 1½×6-inch lattice piece to right of 10½×6-inch background piece. Sew 17½×1½-inch lattice piece to bottom of complete sections 1 and 2.

3. Section 3: Cut 6½×7½-inch rectangle from background fabric and 1¼×7½-inch strip, 1½×7½-inch strip, and 8¼×1¾-inch strip from lattice. Sew 1¼×7½-inch lattice piece to right side of background piece and 1½×7½-inch piece to left side. Sew 8¼×1¾-inch lattice piece to bottom of block.

4. Section 4: Cut 6¼×4¾-inch rectangle from background fabric and 1¼×4¾-inch strip from lattice. Sew lattice piece to right side of background piece.

5. Section 5: Cut 3¼×4¾-inch rectangle from background fabric and 9¾×1¼-inch strip from lattice. Sew background piece to right of block created in Step 4. Sew lattice piece cut in this step to bottom of sections 4 and 5 (with lattice piece between).

6. Section 6: Cut 9¾×3¾-inch rectangle from background fabric. Sew background piece to bottom of block created in Step 5. Sew this block to right of section 3. Sew top and bottom blocks together.

7. Cut seventeen 1½-inch squares from multicolor scraps. Sew squares together to form strip. Sew this strip to bottom of already created block.

8. To make accent border, cut two 1½×17½-inch strips and two 18¼×1½-inch strips from accent border fabric. Sew 1½×17½-inch strips to top and bottom of block. Sew 18¼×1½-inch strips to right and left sides of block.

9. To make outside border, cut two 19½×3½-inch strips and two 3½×24¼-inch strips from outside border fabric. Sew 19½×3½-inch strips to top and bottom of block. Sew 3½×24¼-inch strips to right and left sides of block.

10. Cut backing and batting 2 inches larger than quilt face. Place quilt face on top of backing and batting. Pin baste with 1-inch safety pins. Trim batting and backing even with quilt face.

11. Cut six 2½-inch-wide strips of fabric (selvage to selvage). Follow directions on pages 14–15 to stitch binding to quilt.

12. Iron fusible webbing to wrong side of all appliqué fabrics. Trace patterns on pages 112–113 on paper side of webbing, and cut out patterns (patterns are already reversed). If you are sewing the appliqués by hand, be sure to cut out patterns ½ inch larger than drawn for seam allowance. Remove paper backing. Lay out pieces on quilt, and fuse to quilt. Machine-quilt, buttonhole-stitch, or pen-stitch around pieces. Mark quilting design with washable marking pencil. Starting in center, quilt with small even stitches.

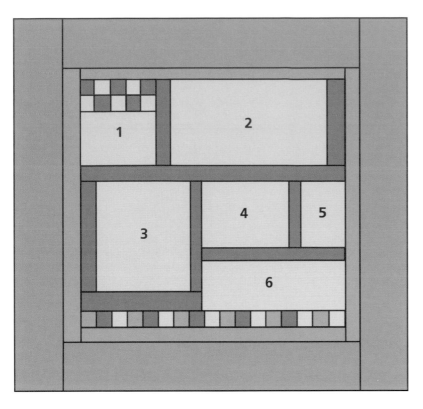

Block 1 and 6 chicken

Patterns are 100%.

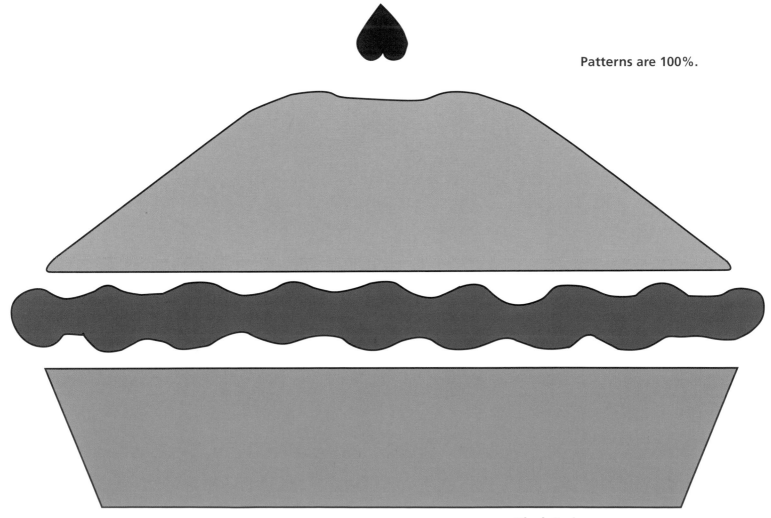

Block 2 pie

Block 4 apple

Block 5 jam jar

Block 4 basket

Block 3 teapot

Patterns are 100%.

Sunflower Garden

Extend the warm colors of rustic country fields with this mixture of yellow sunflowers, orange pumpkins, and burgundy Indian corn.

What You'll Need

- 3½×6½×6½-inch distressed wood crate
- 3×4×4-inch block dry floral foam
- Low-temperature glue gun and glue sticks
- Sheet moss
- 2 to 4 pieces green reindeer moss
- 2 stems mustard yellow silk sunflowers, 4- to 5-inch heads each
- Ruler
- Wire cutters
- Mustard yellow silk sunflower spray with two 2-inch heads and 1 bud
- Sunflower seed packet
- 3-inch silk pumpkin pick
- Burgundy mini Indian corn
- Metal garden spade
- Dried black-eyed Susan head
- 6 to 8 branches green preserved eucalyptus
- 4 to 5 wood branches
- 4 to 5 strands natural raffia

1. Glue foam into crate. Cover with moss.

2. Using wire cutters, trim a large sunflower 21 to 22 inches long, and insert into middle of crate. Cut second large sunflower 15 to 16 inches long, and insert to the right of center. Cut

sunflower off sunflower spray, and trim wire. Cut spray 10 to 12 inches long, and insert into left side of crate.

3. Glue seed packet, trimmed sunflower, pumpkin, and Indian corn into base of crate.

4. Glue end of spade tip into foam at front left of crate. Glue dried flower head onto spade.

5. Cut eucalyptus 16 to 18 inches long, and insert behind sunflowers. Cut shorter pieces of eucalyptus, and insert them around sides of crate. Add other branches throughout arrangement. Tie raffia to spade handle.

SUNFLOWER
GIANT GREYSTRIPE
$1.29

FLEURS

Friendly Witch Next Door

What better way to greet trick-or-treaters than with this friendly witch. What's more, a doll will last a lot longer than all those sweet treats!

What You'll Need

- 18-inch premade muslin doll
- Green acrylic paint
- Paintbrush
- Red permanent fine-tip marker
- Powder blush
- Tracing paper
- Pencil
- Scissors
- ½ yard each black broadcloth, Halloween print
- Ruler
- Sewing machine
- Black thread
- Needle
- Buttons: 5 star, 2 moon or star
- Iron and ironing board
- 24 inches black ribbon, 1/16 inch wide
- Craft glue
- 6-inch black felt witch hat
- Orange ribbon
- Waxed paper
- Glow-in-the-dark dimensional paint: orange, yellow
- Skein orange yarn
- 12×4-inch cardboard hair template

1. Dot 2 green eyes on doll face. Draw smile with permanent red marker. Let dry. Lightly apply powder blush to cheeks.

2. Trace and cut out pattern on page 118. Cut out romper from black broadcloth, and slit along solid fold line. Following pattern instructions, sew with ¼-inch seam allowance. Clip corners, and turn romper right side out. Slip romper on doll through neck opening. Turn raw edges of neckline down ¼ inch, and sew a running stitch around neckline. Knot off.

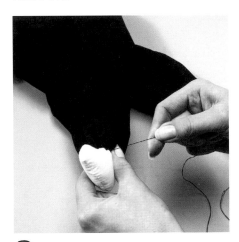

3. Turn sleeves under ¼ inch, and gather with running stitch. Gather at doll's elbow and knot off. Turn pant hems under ¼ inch, and gather with running stitch. Gather at ankle; knot off.

4. Sew 3 star buttons to center front of romper. First button is ½ inch from top of neckline; space buttons 1 inch apart. Sew moon or star buttons to outside bottom of romper legs.

5. Sew side and bottom seams on cape. Fold top raw edge of cape down 1 inch (wrong sides together), and iron crease. Sew a running stitch across cape 1 inch down from top. Gather to neckline. Place cape on doll. To measure, pull gathers until ends surround but don't cover face. Knot off. Sew last 2 star buttons to cape. Cut black ribbon into three 8-inch pieces. Glue ribbons to inside of cape even with star buttons. Let dry.

6. Wrap orange ribbon around base of hat. Tie ribbon into simple bow, and trim ends. Glue ribbon to hat.

7. With leftover black material, cut two 6×7-inch pieces. Place 1 piece onto waxed paper, and write "Trick or Treat" on fabric with orange glow-in-the-dark paint. Dot yellow glow-in-the-dark paint around writing. Let paint dry 24 hours. Fold tops of fabric down 1 inch. With right sides together, sew bag together with ¼-inch seam allowance. Turn bag. Glue last piece of 8-inch ribbon to bag for handle.

8. Wrap yarn around hair template about 20 times, depending on thickness of yarn. Cut one end of yarn from template. Remove 3 strands. Find center of hair and use yarn strand to tie temporary knot at center. Measure 3¼ inches down from center, and tie permanent knot. Repeat for other side. Remove temporary knot. Apply thin line of glue across top of doll's head horizontally. Slightly twist hair between permanent knots, and place hair over glue; hold. Make sure pigtails are balanced on doll's head. Once glue has set, tack hair to doll with needle and thread; knot off. If hair doesn't seem secure, apply more glue under hairline, and hold in place until glue sets.

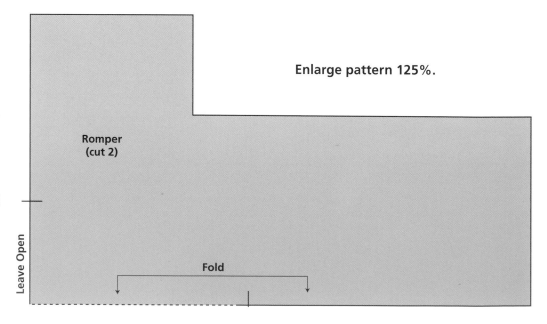

Enlarge pattern 125%.

Romper
(cut 2)

Leave Open

Fold

Winter

*What better way to banish the winter blues than with
the warmth of handmade gifts? With so many winter projects to choose
from, you'll be working far into those cozy winter nights to
create wonderful gifts and decorations.*

Bright Lights Cookie Plate

Give your cookies that extra-special touch by presenting them on a plate decorated with hand-painted Christmas lights.

What You'll Need

- Scissors
- Masking tape
- Clear, smooth 10-inch glass plate
- Enamel paint: black, green, white, yellow, red, blue
- Bottle-tip nozzle pen set
- Foam plate
- 5 paintbrushes, #2 round

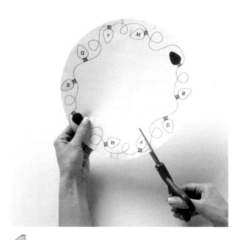

1. Use copier to make 2 copies of pattern on page 123. Cut out patterns along semicircle outline. Flip 1 pattern so ends of cord outline match up with other pattern, creating a continuous circular pattern. Tape in place. Snip ½-inch tabs all around pattern to allow paper to conform to plate. Position and tape pattern facedown on top of glass plate. Design will be painted on bottom of plate.

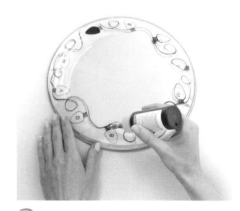

2. Using pen set, attach extension cap and fine metal tip to black enamel bottle. Practice squeezing lines of enamel from bottle onto foam plate, then draw thin black definition lines for sockets and cords and around each bulb. Let dry. (Quickly and thoroughly rinse out cap and metal tip after each use.)

3. Thin small amount of green enamel with water on foam plate. Using pattern as your guide and painting on top of black definition lines, paint a line over coiling cord. Also use green to fill in sockets and 2 green bulbs. Be sure to apply paint strokes in same direction. Let dry, and repeat if necessary to achieve opaque coverage.

4. Thin small amount of white enamel with water, and paint white lightbulbs. Repeat with remaining paint colors to fill in yellow, red, and blue bulbs.

5. Follow manufacturer's instructions on enamel bottles for drying, baking, and curing enamel to glass.

Tip

Painting mistakes can be easily removed by washing them away with water before the paint has completely dried or by scraping the dried enamel off with your fingernail. Remember: Once the enamel has been cured, it becomes permanent.

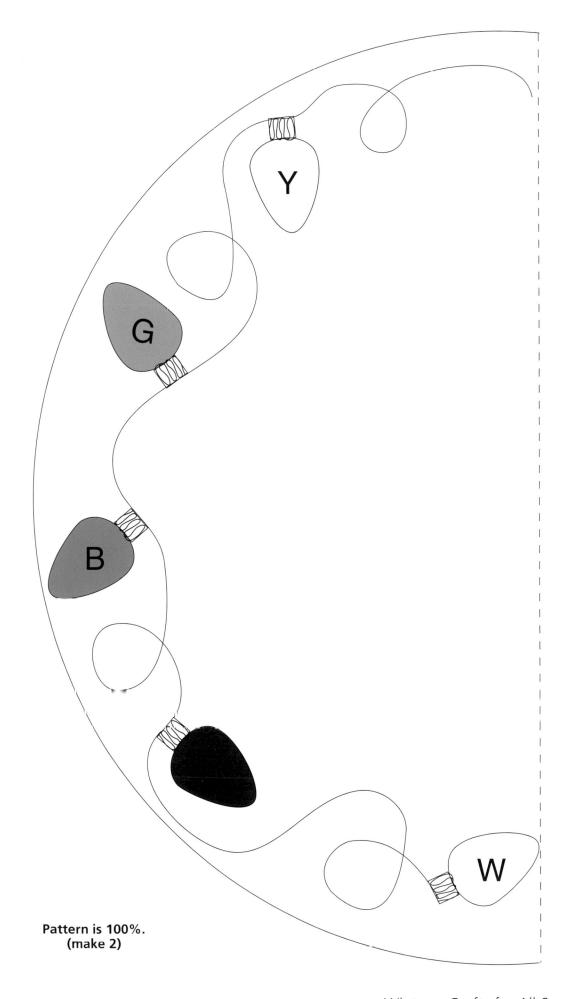

Pattern is 100%.
(make 2)

Santas in a Row Mantel Swag

Santa will be happy to fill your stocking with goodies when he sees his jolly likeness hanging from your mantel!

What You'll Need

- Tracing paper
- Pencil
- Scissors
- Light iron-on adhesive
- Fabric scraps: beige, red, red-and-white print, yellow, white, light gray, pink
- Iron and ironing board
- 3 pieces heavy brown paper, 5×12 inches each
- 3 pieces cream or white heavy felt, 5×6 inches each
- Fabric scissors
- Sewing machine
- Tan thread
- Ruler
- Powder blush
- Fine-tip black pen
- 24 inches jute or hemp string
- Hot glue gun and glue sticks

- 30 to 35 strips assorted Christmas fabric scraps (for ties), 1×7 inches each: prints, plaids, checks

1. Trace and cut out patterns from page 127. Then trace 3 of each pattern onto paper side of iron-on adhesive. Group all the same patterns together (i.e., stars with stars, hats with hats), leaving a little room around each traced pattern.

2. Cut around each group of patterns on the adhesive, leaving a border around each. Place patterns glue side down on wrong sides of fabric scraps as follows: faces on beige, hats on red, hat trims on red-and-white print, stars on yellow, beards on white, mustaches on light gray, and noses on pink. Iron pieces using medium heat and no steam. When cool, peel off paper backing.

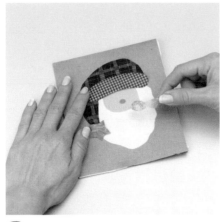

3. Fold each piece of brown paper in half lengthwise, and insert cream or white felt in each. Cut out each of the Santa fabric pieces, and position them onto center of brown paper. Press in place. Repeat for all Santas.

4. With sewing machine and thread, straight stitch around Santa face, following outline. Use a large straight stitch and a very sharp needle to prevent tearing. Repeat for all Santas.

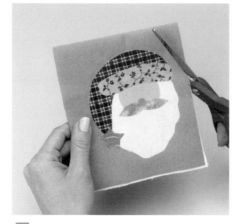

5. Trim ⅛ inch outside stitching for all Santas. Don't cut too close to stitching.

6. Add blush to cheeks with finger, and draw on eyes with fine-tip black pen. Add stitching lines to beard and hat trim. Repeat for all Santas.

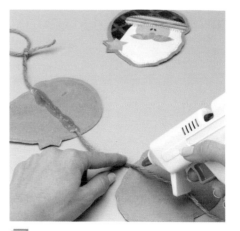

7. Tie loops on both ends of jute for hanging. Glue jute to backs of Santas, placing Santas evenly along length. Leave about 2 to 3 inches between each Santa and between Santas and hanging loops.

8. Tie 6 to 8 Christmas fabric strips between each Santa and on each end. If needed, add more ties to fill up space.

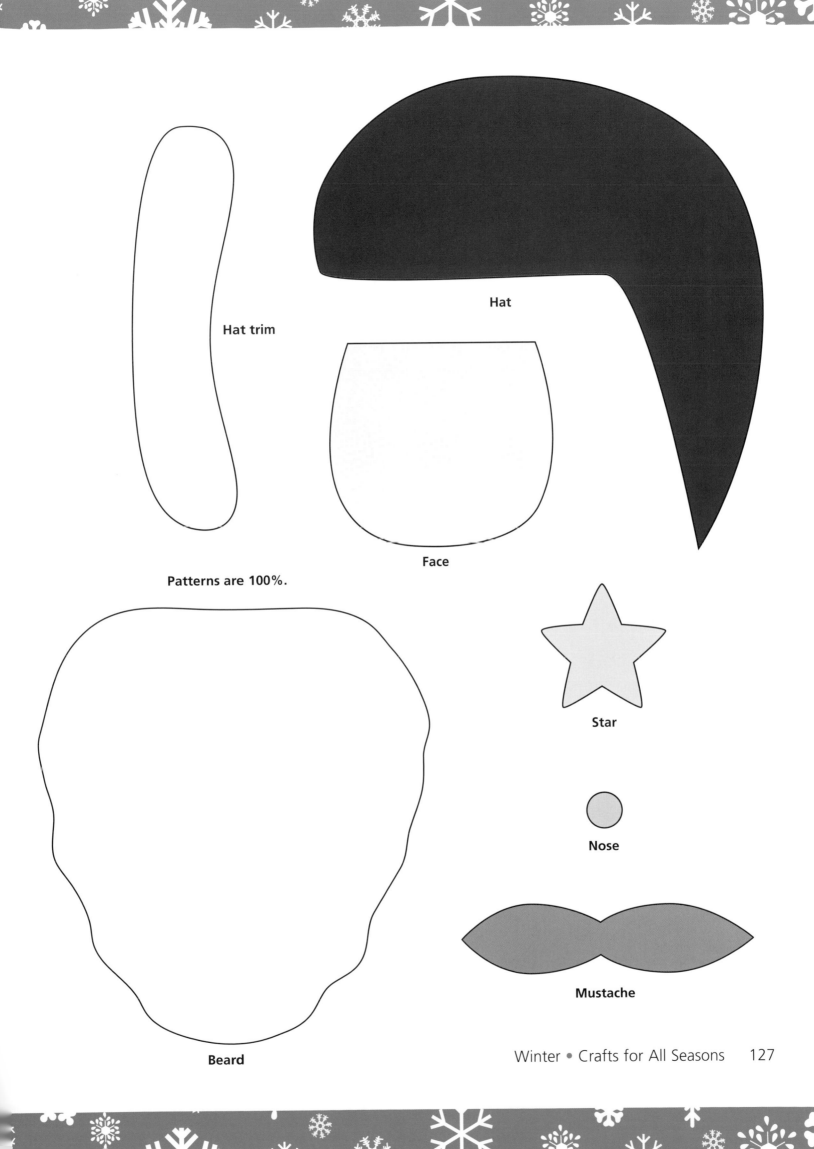

Hat trim

Hat

Face

Patterns are 100%.

Star

Nose

Beard

Mustache

Southern Magnolia Holiday Wreath

The South's most beautiful flower is highlighted on this formal holiday wreath. Elegant ivory magnolias dance through Christmas greenery, glass ornaments, and golden holly leaves.

What You'll Need

- 5 silk magnolias with 4 buds each
- Ruler
- Wire cutters
- Floral wire
- Artificial pine wreath
- Hot glue gun and glue sticks
- 27 gold glass ball ornaments on wire picks, 1 inch each
- 2 gold silk holly branches
- 2 yards sheer wired ribbon
- 10 natural pinecones

1. Cut stems of magnolia flowers to 2 inches. Cut off buds and leaves from stems. Form a collar around flower with leaves, and wrap with floral wire to hold in place. Do the same with buds.

2. Insert magnolias and buds into wreath. Twist pine branches around stems to secure. Add a touch of hot glue for extra security. Space flowers evenly around wreath, leaving room for ornaments.

3. Twist 3 glass balls together to form a cluster. Make 9 clusters. Insert clusters into wreath between magnolias. Twist pine branches around clusters to hold them in place.

4. Cut holly branches into 3- to 4-inch lengths. Glue them into wreath around magnolias. Glue remaining magnolia leaves to hide any wire that shows.

5. Cut ribbon into three 24-inch lengths. Form 2 loops of ribbon, and twist together with floral wire. Secure each ribbon to wreath behind a magnolia. Keep ribbon loops to sides of flowers so flowers remain dominant. Space ribbons evenly around wreath.

6. Glue in pinecones and remaining holly leaves to hide any glue or wire.

Winter Wonderland Mailbox Topper

Send a holiday greeting to all who pass by your home with this sweet snowman mailbox topper.

What You'll Need

- Tape measure
- Blue canvas
- Fabric pen or chalk
- Scissors
- Hot glue gun and glue sticks
- 3 yards blue grosgrain ribbon, ⅝ inch wide
- Kemper tool or old toothbrush
- White paint
- Tracing paper
- Pencil
- Felt: white, red, orange, black
- Fine-tip black pen
- White embroidery floss
- Embroidery needle

1. Measure mailbox length, and add 1 inch. Measure height of one side of mailbox from center top to bottom edge. Double this measurement, and add 1 inch. Cut canvas according to measurements.

2. Turn all edges of canvas under ½ inch, and glue in place with hot glue gun.

3. Cut four 27-inch lengths of grosgrain ribbon. Use glue gun to attach ½ inch of one end of each ribbon to underside of topper at each corner. Trim loose ends diagonally to prevent raveling.

4. To create snowy effect on topper, spatter-paint canvas with Kemper tool and white paint. (You can achieve the same result by loading an old toothbrush with paint and running your thumb across the top of the bristles.) Let dry.

5. Trace and cut out 6 of each pattern on the right as follows: body from white felt, scarf from red, nose from orange, and hat from black. If needed, use fabric pen or chalk to transfer hat pattern to black felt.

6. Lay canvas topper right side up on flat surface. Randomly scatter snowmen on top. When positioned as desired, glue white snowman bodies in place, then add hat, nose, and scarf to each one. Draw black dots for eyes.

Patterns are 100%.

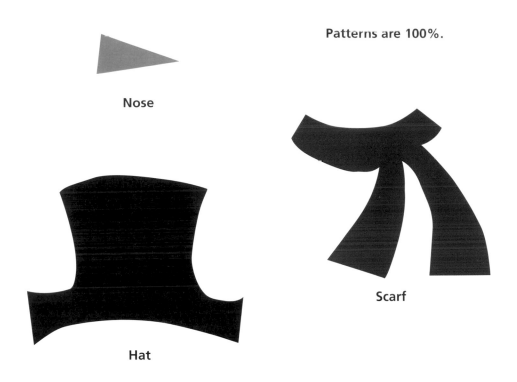

Nose

Scarf

Hat

7. Blanket-stitch front and back edges of topper with white embroidery floss for a finished look. Drape topper over mailbox, and tie ribbons together to secure. Note: Design does not account for mailbox flag, so it cannot be used when topper is in place.

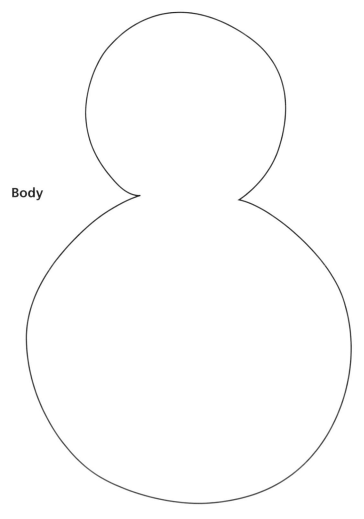

Body

Simply Elegant Trees

"Elegant" is just the right word for this holiday wall hanging. Rich colors and gold accents create an aura of sophisticated charm.

What You'll Need

- Sewing machine
- Quilting needle
- Thread: gold metallic, red, green
- Tracing paper
- Pencil
- Scissors
- Self-healing mat
- See-through ruler
- Rotary cutter
- 30-inch square low-loft polyester batting

Quilt fabrics

- ¼ yard each green print, white-on-white print, dark red print
- ⅛ yard brown
- ½ yard Christmas print
- ¾ yard backing
- ⅓ yard dark green

1. With gold metallic thread, sew embellishing lines on green print fabric from top to bottom. Lines should be graceful curves and may intersect each other.

2. Trace and cut out all pattern pieces on page 134. Trace and cut 6 A triangles from green print. Cut 6 B triangles and 6 B reversed from white-on-white print. Sew triangle B and triangle B reversed to each triangle A to form tree.

3. From brown fabric, cut six 2×2½-inch trunks. From white-on-white print, cut twelve 2½×2¾-inch rectangles. Sew 2 white rectangles to either side of each brown trunk along 2½-inch sides. Sew trunk sections to bottom of tree sections to form blocks.

4. Cut two 2½×45-inch strips from Christmas print. Cut strips into four 8-inch strips and three 6-inch strips. Cut two 2½-inch squares from dark red print.

5. Stitch together 2 rows of 3 trees each separated by Christmas print sashing and corner blocks (see finished quilt photo).

6. Cut three 1½×45-inch strips from dark red print. Measure quilt vertically through center, and cut 2 strips to this length from one of the long strips. Stitch to sides. Measure quilt horizontally through center. Use remaining strips to make border for top and bottom.

7. Cut three 2½×45 inch strips from Christmas print. Measure quilt vertically through center, and cut 2 strips to this length from one of the long strips. Stitch to sides. Use remaining strips to make border for top and bottom.

8. Layer front, batting, and back; baste. Quilt in ditches around trees with gold metallic thread. Quilt in ditches around blocks and borders with red thread. Cut three 2¾×45-inch strips from dark green print. Follow directions on pages 14–15 to stitch binding to quilt, using green thread.

Enlarge patterns 120%.

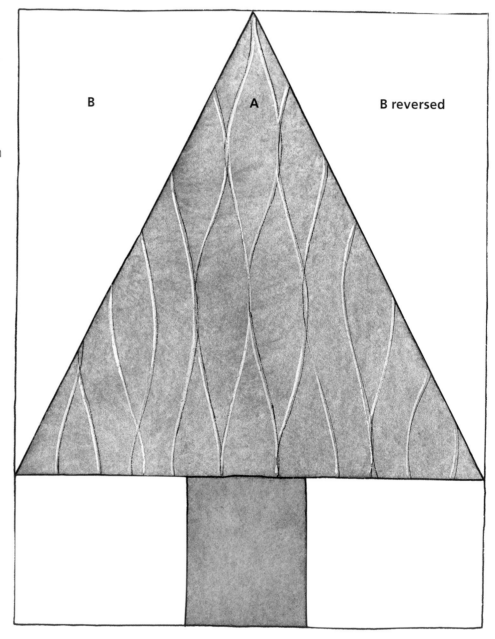

Holiday Treat Recipe Cards

Write your favorite Christmas recipes on these homemade cards for that extra-special gift-giving touch!

What You'll Need

- Tracing paper
- Soft-lead pencil
- Scissors
- Eraser carving material
- Cutting surface or board
- Craft knife
- #21 blade linoleum cutter
- Ink pads: dark red, dark green
- Scrap paper
- 12 off-white cards, 4×6 inches each
- Ruler
- Dark red colored pencil
- 24 inches twine

1. Trace patterns on page 137 with soft-lead pencil; cut out. Transfer designs to eraser carving material by placing paper facedown and rubbing back of image with your thumbnail.

2. On cutting surface or board, cut 2 images apart with craft knife. Use linoleum cutter to cut out patterns.

Tip

As you cut eraser carving material, turn carving material rather than moving the cutter.

3. Trim away excess from 2 images with craft knife, slanting cut away from image.

4. Using dark red and dark green ink pads, test images by stamping on scrap paper. Trim again if needed.

5. On each of the 12 cards, stamp tree in dark green at each end and in middle along bottom. Stamp heart in red between trees.

6. Use ruler and dark red pencil to mark off 5 lines ½ inch apart on each card, starting ½ inch from top. If desired, mark off lines on reverse as well.

7. Bundle cards, and tie with twine.

Patterns are 100%.

Country Folk Santa

This folk art Santa is sure to fly into your heart and become part of your family holiday traditions. Make several to give as wonderful handmade gifts!

What You'll Need

- 1-inch pine board
- Stylus
- Graphite paper
- Jigsaw
- Sandpaper
- Tack cloth
- Drill and small drill bit
- Ruler
- Waterbase varnish
- Acrylic paint: cream, black, red, green
- Paintbrushes: 4 small flat, 10/0 liner, small foam
- Kemper tool
- Jute
- Scissors
- Craft glue

Tip

If you don't have a jigsaw, you can have your local lumber store cut out the shapes for you.

1. Transfer patterns on page 140 to wood using stylus and graphite paper.

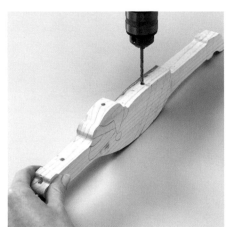

2. Cut out Santa and bag from wood. Sand until smooth, and use tack cloth to remove dust. Drill 2 holes through thickness of wood—one in top of hands and another approximately 1½ inches closer to head. Make sure holes are completely through. Also drill holes through bag, the same distance apart as holes in arms. Drill 2 shallow holes on top edge of Santa (about ¼ inch deep).

3. Mix varnish with each color of acrylic paint to make a stain. Test on sample wood for proper transparency. Wrap color around edge, or thickness, of wood. Leave Santa's face bare. Paint fur, beard, and candy cane cream. Use black for belt and boots and red for suit, ball, and candy stripe. Paint gloves and bag green. Let paint dry.

4. Line entire pattern with black.

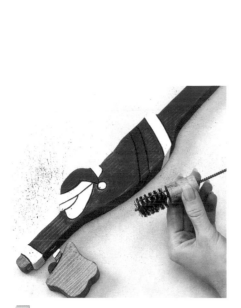

5. Spatter-paint front and thicknesses of wood with black and Kemper tool.

6. Use foam brush to finish entire surface with varnish.

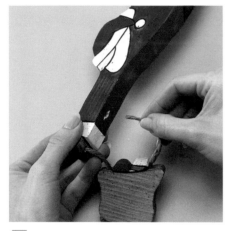

7. Cut two 4-inch pieces of jute. Tie knot in one end, then thread jute from bag bottom through drilled hole. Continue through hands; tie knot in end. Repeat with second piece of jute, threading through other hole in bag and arm. For hanger, cut 12-inch piece of jute. Tie tight bow in center. Insert glue in shallow drilled holes, and push jute ends in holes; let dry.

Enlarge pattern 130%.

Pattern is 100%.

A Ring of Angels

*Encircle your Christmas tree with a crowd of angels!
You'll be glad you did—especially when it
is time to clean up the fallen needles.*

What You'll Need

- 54-inch round felt hunter green tablecloth
- Tape measure
- Pencil
- Fabric scissors
- Iron and ironing board
- 2 yards fabric adhesive
- Felt squares: 3 antique white, 2 yellow, 3 red
- ½ yard gold lamé
- Tracing paper
- Scissors
- Dimensional fabric paint: gold, gold glitter, ivory, green glitter
- Paintbrushes: two #8 flat, two 10/0 liner
- 5 yards small gold rickrack
- Fabric glue
- Acrylic paint: rose, black
- 2 yards thin gold cord
- 8 yards fancy gold trim, ¾ inch wide

1. Cut a straight line to center of tablecloth. Cut out a 4-inch circle for tree.

2. Iron adhesive to back of felt squares and lamé, using medium setting. Press 4 to 5 seconds. Trace and cut out patterns on page 142. Trace patterns onto paper backing. Skirt will have 5 angels holding 5 stars plus 30 scattered stars. Use antique white for face, hands, feet; yellow for hair; red for dress; and gold lamé for stars. Cut out, and remove paper.

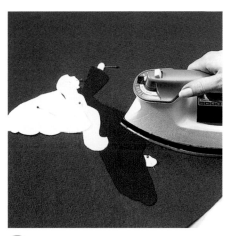

3. Position first angel on skirt. Iron appliqués to felt. Evenly space remaining angels around skirt, and adhere. Iron on both shapes of stars. Spread gold fabric paint over wings with flat brush.

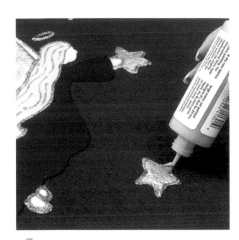

4. Outline hair, stars, and wings with gold glitter paint. Draw on shoes and halo with gold glitter. Outline face and hands with ivory using liner brush.

5. Glue gold rickrack around dresses and sleeves. Glue rickrack across dresses.

6. Lightly paint cheeks with rose acrylic paint and flat brush. Using liner brush and black, paint eyes. Draw holly on dress with green glitter paint, and dot around holly and dot buttons on sleeve with ivory. Divide gold cord into 10 pieces. Tie 2 bows for each angel, and glue 1 bow to waist and 1 bow at tail of dress. Glue trim around skirt and center hole. Let dry.

Patterns are 100%.

Holiday Pear Garland

Faux green pears trim a garland of assorted greenery, berries, natural birch twigs, and golden holly leaves. Place this lovely arrangement over a doorway, let it cascade down a staircase, or use it to adorn a table.

What You'll Need

- 22-gauge stem floral wire
- Ruler
- Wire cutters
- 36 faux pears
- Brown floral tape
- 8 green berry stems
- 5 silk lemon leaf stems
- 2 pine sprays with gold glitter
- Natural birch branches
- 9-foot silk pine garland
- 2 gold holly sprays
- Hot glue gun and glue sticks

1. Cut floral wire into 6-inch lengths. Extend stem ends of pears with floral wire by covering wire and stem with brown floral tape. Set aside. Cut berry stems, lemon leaf stems, and pine sprays into 4- to 5-inch lengths. Set aside.

2. Place birch branches in pine garland, and twist pine branches around birch to hold in place. Use floral wire if needed for extra security. Birch branches should extend 4 to 5 inches from garland.

3. Use floral wire to add berry sprays, pine sprays, and lemon leaf sprays to garland.

4. Add pears by twisting stem ends into garland. Add extra branches, berries, and other leaves as needed to give garland a full and lush look.

5. Cut holly sprays into small pieces, and glue into garland. Use them to hide any wire that shows.

Try This!

- For a novel approach, add feathered partridges to remind guests of the 12 days of Christmas. Tuck in ribbons or small bows for added texture and color.
- Coordinate a holiday party theme with your garland. Make place cards for each dinner guest by cutting a small slit into the top of a faux pear and tucking in a small card with a guest's name on it.

Fanciful Stemware Charms

These sparkling wine charms are sure to be a hit at your next holiday gathering. Simple to make, consider creating several sets to give as gifts.

What You'll Need

- 2.1 ounces white air-dry clay
- Freezer paper
- Clay roller
- Small clay cutters
- Mini Christmas stamps
- Gold eye pins
- Gold acrylic paint
- #2 round paintbrush
- Small foam block
- Metallic jewel-tone plated beads in various shapes and sizes
- Needlenose pliers
- 10 yards gold craft wire, 20 gauge
- Ruler
- Wire cutters

1. On freezer paper, roll out clay to about ¼ inch thick. Use clay cutters to make shapes out of clay for the number of charms you wish to make.

2. Impress stamp design into center of each shape. Carefully pierce gold eye pin through each shape from top to bottom. Turn pin so eye of pin is facing to the side. (Be careful: The clay will be soft and can become misshapen if handled too firmly.) Let dry overnight.

3. Paint entire surface of shapes with 2 to 3 coats of gold acrylic paint, letting dry between coats. Insert ends of pins into foam block to help paint dry on all sides after each coat.

4. Holding head of eye pin, thread bead on pin at bottom of clay shape. Using needlenose pliers, tightly twist and coil bottom end of pin to just below bead, securing charm and bead near top. Repeat for all charm shapes.

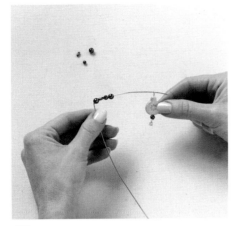

5. Cut 10-inch length of gold wire. Thread large round bead at one end of wire length. Using pliers, wrap end of wire around bead to secure. At opposite end of wire, bend wire into a right angle 3 inches in from end. Using the same bead color, thread another large round bead up to right angle. Thread on beads in this sequence: rice-shape bead, small round bead, large round bead, charm shape with matching color bead, large round bead, small round bead, and rice-shape bead.

6. Bend 3-inch section of beaded wire into gentle loop, meeting wire end to first large bead at right angle. With pliers,

slightly bend ⅛ inch of end of wire, and insert it alongside threaded wire in large round bead hole. Make sure end is firmly and securely held in place by bead.

7. Repeat steps 5 and 6 for remaining charms.

8. Coil wire charms around stemware, and adjust to desired height and form.

Holly Table Runner

It's the small touches that can create the most beauty in a room. This quilted table runner is sure to be that spark to your yuletide decorating.

What You'll Need

- Self-healing mat
- See-through ruler
- Rotary cutter
- 1½ yards fusible adhesive
- Iron and ironing board
- Tracing paper
- Pencil
- Scissors
- Fabric scissors
- Straight pins
- 17×50-inch piece low-loft polyester batting
- Large basting needle
- Thread: ivory, green, red
- Sewing machine
- Quilting needle

Quilt fabrics

- 1½ yards muslin or neutral tone-on-tone print
- ¼ yard each Christmas print, green
- ½ yard red

Refer to page 12 for instructions on how to miter corners.

1. Cut two 17×50-inch pieces from muslin. From Christmas print, cut three 2×45-inch strips.

2. Cut two 9×17-inch pieces of fusible adhesive. Following manufacturer's directions, iron them side by side onto wrong side of green fabric. Trace and cut out holly leaf pattern from page 151. Trace 66 holly leaves onto paper backing of green. Cut out, and remove paper backing.

3. Cut two 18×17-inch pieces of fusible adhesive. Iron them side by side onto wrong side of red. Trace and cut out swag, bow, and holly berry patterns from page 151. Trace 6 swags, 8 bows, and 33 holly berries onto paper backing of red. Cut out, and remove paper backing.

4. Center wreath guide on muslin, and lightly trace around it. Trace a circle with wreath guide on each end, 6½ inches from end and 4 inches from each side.

5. Pin 11 holly leaves end to end on each wreath guide circle. End points of leaves should touch pencil line. Fuse.

6. Using photo as your guide, line up 11 more holly leaves on each wreath. Fuse last 11 holly berries on each wreath between rows of holly leaves.

7. Evenly space swags around wreaths 1 inch from side edges of muslin. Fuse.

8. Center bows between and on ends of swags with bottom points 1 inch from muslin side edges. Fuse.

9. Sandwich batting between top and second piece of muslin, with right sides out. Pin along perimeter. Hand-baste through all thicknesses vertically, horizontally, and around perimeter close to edge. Remove all pins.

10. Set sewing machine for a medium-width zigzag stitch, close enough for an outline satin stitch. Starting with green thread, stitch around edge of each holly leaf, quilting all layers together.

11. Change to red thread, and follow the same procedure to stitch holly berries, swags, and bows. When stitching is complete, remove all basting stitches except perimeter.

12. Stitch binding strips together to make a very long 2-inch strip. Follow directions on pages 14–15 to stitch binding to quilt. Miter corners.

Bow

Wreath guide

Fold

Holly berry

Patterns are 100%.

Holly leaf

Swag

Country Cute Christmas Ornaments

These delightful ornaments will add a special touch to your Christmas tree. Use leftover trims and ribbon you have around the house—you'll be surprised at how creative you can be!

What You'll Need

- Precut wood tree ornaments
- Acrylic paint: gold, green, brown, yellow, white, metallic gold
- Paintbrushes: six #8 shaders, 10/0 liner
- Low-temperature glue gun and glue sticks
- Trims: assorted lengths of white and gold rickrack, material strips, red satin ribbon, gold trim, off-white rattail cord, cream sheer ribbon, ribbon roses, gold cord
- Scissors
- Sparkle glaze
- Assorted buttons
- Precut ¾-inch wood star
- Kemper tool or old toothbrush
- Decorative snow
- Floral accents: pale gold glitter spray, pale gold highlighter
- Acrylic spray sealer

1. Paint some tree ornaments gold and some green. Paint tree trunks brown.

2. Child's Tree: Glue rickrack to tree; paint with sparkle glaze. Let dry. Glue on pastel buttons. Tie a rickrack bow around hanger.

3. Country Tree: Paint wood star yellow. Tie rag bow; glue to wire hanger. Glue star to tree. Glue burgundy and small white buttons to tree. Using liner brush and white paint, write "Noel" on trunk. Use Kemper tool or old paintbrush to spatter-paint ornament with white paint. Let dry.

4. Antique Memories Button Tree: Tie a red satin bow, and glue to wire hanger. Glue on 4 old buttons, and spatter-paint tree with white paint. Dab snow with shader brush on tree and top of buttons. Let dry.

5. **Victorian Bridal Tree:** Glue gold trim and off-white rattail cording to tree. Tie small bow of cream sheer ribbon to hanger. Glue ribbon rose to top of tree. Glue cream buttons to tree. Mist with pale gold glitter spray. Let dry.

6. **Traditional Gold Tree:** Glue gold rickrack to tree. Make bow out of gold cord; glue to top of tree. Glue buttons to tree. Mist with pale gold highlighter. Let dry. Add dots using paintbrush end dipped into metallic gold paint. Let dry.

7. Mist all ornaments with acrylic spray sealer.

Jolly Jingle Bell Candleholder

Bring the spirit of holiday music into your home with this festive candleholder. Group a few together to create a wonderful centerpiece, or give as a gift to your favorite holiday host.

What You'll Need

- 9-inch-tall clear glass cylindrical vase with 3¼-inch opening
- 2×2 inches foam
- Low-temperature glue gun and glue sticks
- 8 evergreen sprigs, 6 inches each
- Wire cutters
- Scissors
- 3 sheet music pages
- 1 yard gold metallic ribbon, 1¾ inches wide
- Ruler
- Floral wire
- 2 red berry sprays, 12 inches each
- 6 holly leaves
- 48 gold jingle bells, assorted sizes
- Clear glass votive holder
- Red votive candle

1. Glue foam block to bottom outside of vase. This is where you will insert evergreens.

2. Place vase so foam block is on your right side. Insert and glue 2 evergreen sprigs horizontally at base of foam, one coming in front of foam and one extending away from foam. Cut evergreens into short lengths, and fill in around already inserted evergreens.

3. Cut pages of sheet music in half horizontally. Tightly roll each section, and glue edges in place to secure. Cut 1 music roll in half, and insert and glue all rolled pages into evergreens.

4. About 6 inches from one end of gold ribbon, shape 2 loops about 3½ inches each. Pinch 2 loops together, and secure with short length of floral wire. Trim end of bow streamers to 4 inches, and cut V shape into end of each. Glue remaining ribbon trailing out back of design. Trim end of ribbon into V shape.

5. Cut 1 red berry spray in half, and insert a length vertically behind bow. Insert other section coming forward beneath bow. Cut other berry spray into short lengths, and insert around bow. Glue holly leaves into design around bow and music. Glue jingle bell to middle of bow; add more jingle bells as desired.

6. Fill vase with assorted jingle bells to about 3 inches from top. Place votive holder with candle inside vase.

Sweet Snowman Stack Boxes

This captivating cutie can hold candy or small surprises for visitors, or it would look just as charming on a table—keeping you company all winter long!

What You'll Need

- 3 hatboxes: 2×3½ inches, 5×2½ inches, 3×5½ inches
- Acrylic paint: white, blue, purple, orange, yellow, fuchsia, black
- Paintbrushes: 4 sponge, liner, ½-inch flat
- 1½-inch wood knob with flat bottom
- ½-inch wood button
- Pencil
- Hot glue gun and glue sticks
- 5 buttons, ⅝ inch each: 2 fuchsia, 2 green, 1 yellow

1. With a sponge brush, paint all hatboxes and lids white. Let dry. Use sponge brushes to paint medium lid blue, small lid and wood knob purple, and ½-inch button orange. Let lids, knob, and button dry. If needed, apply another coat of paint.

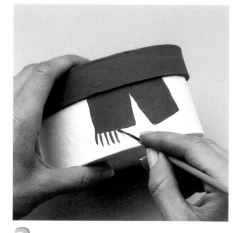

2. Use pencil to lightly draw scarf on medium hatbox. Paint scarf blue. Let dry. (Paint another coat if needed.) With liner brush, paint blue fringe on bottom edge of scarf. Let dry.

3. Make dots on scarf and medium lid with yellow paint and paintbrush end. Let dry.

4. Glue orange button to center of small hatbox for nose. Add cheeks using fuchsia paint and flat brush. Dot eyes and mouth with black paint and paintbrush end. Let dry.

5. Glue wood knob to center top of small lid. Glue buttons to center front of medium hatbox, large lid, and large hatbox as shown.

Candy-Coated Christmas Wreath

You will see visions of sugarplums dancing in your head when you make this sparkling holiday wreath. Assorted miniature fruit, berries, and minty candy canes glisten with a "candy coating" of diamond dust.

What You'll Need

- 54 pieces artificial fruit on wire picks
- Craft glue
- Small artist's paintbrush
- Diamond dust or opalescent glitter
- 2 red berry stems
- 2 dozen plastic candy canes
- 14-inch artificial pine wreath
- Wire cutters
- Hot glue gun and glue sticks

Tip

When you store your wreath from year to year, some of the diamond dust might come off. You can easily touch up the wreath by brushing the pieces of fruit with a little more glue and adding a fresh sprinkling of diamond dust.

1. With small artist's paintbrush, coat each piece of fruit with glue. Sprinkle diamond dust over fruit pieces. Repeat process on berries and candy canes. Let dry overnight.

2. Shape evergreen wreath by pulling out and fluffing branches.

3. Twist 3 pieces of different fruit together into a cluster. Place fruit clusters into wreath. Twist stems of fruit into branches. Continue around wreath until it is full.

4. Cut each berry stem into about 5 pieces; each piece should have approximately 5 berries. Glue berry stems into wreath. Spread berries throughout wreath.

5. Glue candy canes into wreath at an angle so they stick out from fruits and berries.

Try This!

For a variation, add a bow to this sparkling confection. Choose a soft color for the ribbon so it doesn't take away from the pastels of the fruit. A small bow with a few streamers tied at the bottom would look best.

Index